100% Information Literacy Success

100% Information LITERACY SUCCESS

TERRY TAYLOR, PHD

CONTRIBUTING AUTHORS:
JOAN ARTH, AMY SOLOMON, MS, OTR, AND NAOMI WILLIAMSON

THOMSON
DELMAR LEARNING

Australia Brazil Canada Mexico Singapore Spain United Kingdom United States

100% Information Literacy Success

Terry Taylor, PhD • Joan Arth • Amy Solomon, MS, OTR • Naomi Williamson

Vice President, Career Education SBU:
Dawn Gerrain

Director of Learning Solutions:
John Fedor

Managing Editor:
Robert L. Serenka, Jr.

Acquisitions Editor:
Martine Edwards

Product Manager:
Jennifer Anderson

Editorial Assistant:
Falon Ferraro

Director of Production:
Wendy A. Troeger

Production Manager:
Mark Bernard

Content Project Manager:
Karin Jaquays

Art Director:
Joy Kocsis

Technology Project Manager:
Sandy Charette

Director of Marketing:
Wendy E. Mapstone

Channel Manager:
Gerard McAvey

Marketing Coordinator:
Jonathan Sheehan

Cover Design:
Suzanne Nelson

Printed in the United States
4 5 XXX 10 09 08

For more information contact Thomson Delmar Learning, Executive Woods, 5 Maxwell Drive, Clifton Park, NY 12065-2919.

Or find us on the World Wide Web at
www.thomsonlearning.com, www.delmarlearning.com, or www.earlychilded.delmar.com

Library of Congress Cataloging-in-Publication Data

Taylor, Terry.
100% information literacy success / Terry Taylor; contributing authors, Joan Arth . . . [et al.].
p. cm.
Includes indexes.
ISBN 1-4180-4818-6
1. Information literacy—Study and teaching (Higher) 2. Library orientation for college students. 3. Libraries and the Internet. 4. Libraries and colleges. 5. Internet in higher education. I. Arth, Joan. II. Title. III. Title: One hundred percent information literacy success.
ZA3075.T394 2007
028.7071—dc22

2007008898

NOTICE TO THE READER

Find It Fast

Contents

About the Authors

TERRY TAYLOR, PhD

Terry Taylor has been involved in higher education at the post-secondary level for 21 years in several teaching and administrative positions. Since 1985, she has served in a variety of teaching and administrative positions at Denver Technical College, including Department Head for Sports Medicine Technology and Allied Health Programs, Dean of Students, Director of Curriculum, and Director of Advanced Training. She also was Director of New Product Development for DeVry Inc., responsible for researching and developing new products for DeVry Universities, Keller Graduate School of Management, and the Becker CPA Review.

Currently, Dr. Taylor is President of Quantum Integrations, a privately held curriculum development and faculty development company and serves as an adjunct professor, teaching nutrition and science courses for Colorado Community Colleges Online. She speaks nationally on curriculum, accreditation, and faculty development topics. Her range of positions and experiences allows a unique understanding of the business side of the career school sector as well as the challenges facing administrators and faculty in providing quality education to students.

JOAN ARTH

Joan Arth is a K–5 library media specialist who has been with the Liberty Public School District, Liberty, Missouri, for 21 years. She also works as a part-time reference librarian at Maple Woods Community College, Kansas City, Missouri. Active in professional organizations, she has presented workshops on information literacy skills at local, state and national levels. Ms. Arth also serves on the advisory council of the Central Missouri State University Children's Literature Festival.

AMY SOLOMON, MS, OTR

Amy Solomon has been a successful program director and faculty member in career school, community college, and clinical occupational therapy settings. She is an accreditation evaluator for the Accreditation Council for Occupational Therapy Education (ACOTE) and has supervised and coached academic and clinical faculty. Having authored, edited, and reviewed textbooks in addition to developing academic programs and courses, Ms. Solomon's experience contributes to a thorough understanding of curriculum that translates the needs of industry to the classroom. Her understanding of adult learners, combined with her education, accreditation, and faculty development background, result in highly effective learning materials.

NAOMI WILLIAMSON

Naomi Williamson is an Associate Professor of Library Services at Central Missouri State University, where she is the librarian for special collections, which includes the Philip A. Sadler Research Collection of Literature for Children and Young Adults, and the children and young adult collections, which support the teacher education program at the university. She is the director of the annual Children's Literature Festival, in its 39th year, where 5,500 children and 1,300 adults meet with more than 40 children's book authors and illustrators. Ms. Williamson teaches a graduate class on library materials for the Library Science and Information Services program in the Department of Educational Leadership and Human Development.

Preface

CONGRATULATIONS!

Your enrollment in college says that you have made a decision to grow and develop as a person and professional. Your college experience and your future professional activities will require you to locate, evaluate, organize, and communicate information in carrying out your responsibilities and achieving your professional goals. *100% Information Literacy* will provide you with tools to accomplish your objectives.

HOW WILL THIS TEXT HELP ME?

100% Information Literacy discusses skills that are fundamental to becoming an information-literate student and professional, which in turn will contribute to your academic and career success. The text is divided into the following topics: *An Introduction to Information Literacy, Determining the Information You Need, Finding and Accessing Information, Evaluating Information, Organizing Information,* and concluding with Legal and Ethical Issues Related to Information. Use the following summaries of these sections to get an overview of the book and to determine how each topic supports you in the development of information literacy skills.

- *Defining information:* You will be introduced to the concept of information literacy and why it is important to academic and career success. The abundance and rapid flow of data in the Information Era requires understanding, finding, using, evaluating, and communicating information effectively and efficiently in all fields of study.

- *Understanding Information Resources:* You will become familiar with common and more obscure information resources available to you in libraries and on the Internet and how to use them.
- *Finding Information Sources:* Here you will learn how to locate and access information sources from a variety of sources so that you can effectively solve problems and answer questions for school and workplace situations.
- *Evaluating Information:* Because anyone can publish anything on the Internet, you will have to know how to evaluate and determine the credibility of Internet information. You will learn how to evaluate whether an Internet information source is credible and appropriate for your needs. In addition, you will learn how to assess an author's expertise, as well as the currency and relevancy of print and other resources.
- *Organizing Information:* As a professional, you will have to be able to logically organize the information you find so you can use it for your information needs and communicate it to others. Effectively organized information will enable you to accomplish your communication goals.
- *Communicating Information:* Finally, you will explore the many ways that students and professionals communicate information to others. You will become familiar with channels of communication and guidelines for communicating effectively in a variety of professional settings. The emphasis is on using information ethically and legally, and acknowledging others correctly for their intellectual property.

HOW TO USE THIS BOOK

100% Information Literacy is designed to actively involve you in developing information literacy skills. The text includes the following features that will guide you through the material and provide opportunities for you to practice what you've learned.

- *The "Big Picture":* The "Big Picture," provided at the beginning of each chapter, gives you an overview of chapter contents related to the other chapters in the text. As you read through the material, you are encouraged to recognize and consider the relationships between the various concepts and information.

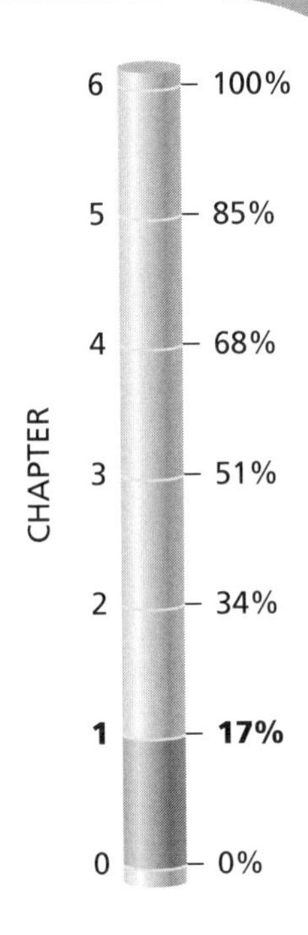

- *Learning Objectives:* Learning Objectives, like those provided on course syllabi, are provided to outline what you should be learning from the chapter and guide you to the main concepts of the chapter. Use the objectives to identify important points and to understand what you are supposed to learn, to measure what you have mastered, and to identify what you still need to work on. You are encouraged to expand your knowledge beyond the learning objectives according to your goals and interests.
- *Topic Scenarios:* At the beginning of each chapter, a Topic Scenario demonstrates the application of chapter concepts to the real world. Use the questions following each scenario to stimulate your critical thinking and analytical skills. Discuss the questions with classmates. You are encouraged to think of your own application of ideas and to raise additional questions.
- *Reflection Questions:* The Reflection Questions ask you to evaluate your personal development. They are intended to increase your self-awareness and ability to understand your decisions and actions.
- *Critical Thinking Questions:* The Critical Thinking Questions challenge you to examine ideas and thoughtfully apply concepts presented in the text. These questions encourage the development of thinking skills that are crucial for efficient performance in school and in the workplace.
- *Learning Activities:* At the end of each chapter are activities that will help you apply the concepts discussed in practical situations. Your instructor may assign these activities as part of the course requirements. Or, if they are not formally assigned, you will want to complete them for your own development:

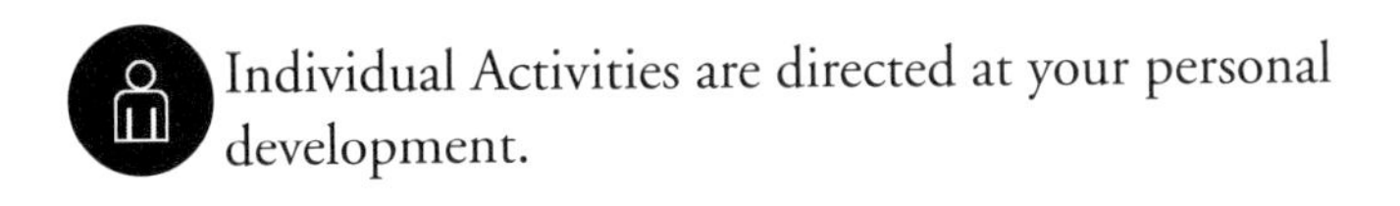
Individual Activities are directed at your personal development.

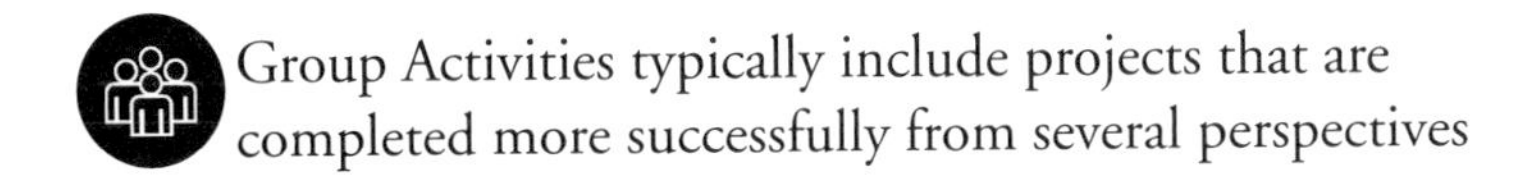
Group Activities typically include projects that are completed more successfully from several perspectives

REFLECTION QUESTION

1. Review the following quote: "In this knowledge-oriented workplace, information literacy is the key to power." What does this mean to you in your own career path? Write down some specific examples of how this might be true for you.

CRITICAL THINKING QUESTIONS

1. An obsolete employee is one who no longer has the skills required to do the job. What specifically might an obsolete employee in your career field look like in ten years?
2. How do ambitious employees prevent themselves from becoming obsolete? Be specific, and relate your ideas specifically to your field of study.

or broader research. As the title suggests, a team effort will contribute to the success of these learning projects.

Internet Activities are intended to help you develop online skills. For example, you may research a topic or participate in an online discussion thread.

You may find it helpful to combine individual and group activities. Some individual activities can be adapted to group activities, and vice versa. Use the activities as guides and modify them in ways that best support your learning.

- *Success Steps:* Scattered throughout the text are Success Steps that offer a pathway to achieve various goals. They essentially summarize the detailed processes that are discussed fully in the body of the text. To achieve a specific information literacy goal, use the *Table of Contents* to locate the information quickly.
- *Learning Objectives Revisited:* Learning Objectives Revisited provides an opportunity for you to assess the effectiveness of your learning and to set goals that will expand your knowledge in a given area. The Learning Objective Revisited grid and instructions for its use are found at the end of each chapter. The following example is taken from chapter 1.

1 = did not achieve objective successfully
2 = understand what is needed but need more study or practice
3 = achieved learning objective thoroughly

	1	2	3
Define Information literacy.	☐	☐	☐
List the specific skills required for an individual to be an information-literate student or professional.	☐	☐	☐
Explain the importance of knowing how to locate, access, retrieve, evaluate, use, and effectively communicate information in school and in the workplace.	☐	☐	☐
Explain the challenges facing an individual who does not possess information skills in school and in the workplace.	☐	☐	☐

Steps to Achieve Unmet Objectives

Steps	Due Date
1. ______	______
2. ______	______
3. ______	______
4. ______	______

- *Developing Portfolios:* A *portfolio* is a collection of the work that you have done. A *learning portfolio* is used to track your progress through school. A *professional portfolio* showcases your professional accomplishments. Throughout *100% Information Literacy Success* you will find numerous suggestions for items to include in a learning portfolio representative of your development and accomplishments in information literacy. Select items for your portfolio from the recommendations at the end of each chapter and include other ideas that reflect your growth in information literacy, and arrange them in a way that illustrates your academic and professional development.

  Use this portfolio to demonstrate to future employers your expertise in information. Consider adding to your portfolio after you have graduated and embarked on a career. As you soon will discover, information literacy will require your continued development to keep up with technological advances. A portfolio is an excellent way to organize and plan for activities that will lead to your continued success in information literacy throughout your working life.

- *100% Information Literacy Online Companion:* This text is supported by additional resources in the Online Companion. These include additional activities, assessments, and suggestions for expanding your knowledge and skills beyond what is included in the text. Access the online companion at http://www.delmarlearning.com/companions/ and search by author (Taylor) or title (100% Information Literacy Success)

A FINAL WORD

Look ahead. As you read and complete the activities in *100% Information Literacy,* keep your long-term goals in mind and think about how you can apply these concepts to your everyday activities. Application is the key—and the more you practice, the more proficient you will become in using and communicating information.

Acknowledgments

The authors of the *100% Success Series* thank the staff at Thomson Delmar Learning for their tireless support and editorial suggestions. Much appreciation also goes to our students over the years who have taught us so much. Without them, this book would not have been possible. We also recognize the many educators and students who reviewed various components of *100% Success* throughout its development and contributed many thoughtful suggestions to the program.

The following individuals contributed significantly to the development of this text. Their efforts and expertise are greatly appreciated.

Kim R. Barnett-Johnson
Ivy Tech Community College
Fort Wayne, Indiana

Katheleene L. Bryan
Daytona Beach Community College
Daytona Beach, Florida

Janet M. Cutshall
Sussex County Community College
Newton, New Jersey

Marianne Fitzpatrick
Oregon Coast Community College
Newport, Oregon

Mark W. Forquer
Advanced Career Training
Jacksonville, Florida

Barbara Ginzburg
Washburn University Law Library
Topeka, Kansas

Cheryl Hollatz-Wisely
Portland State University
Portland, Oregon

Linda Krupovich
Allied Medical and Technical Institute
Forty Fort, Pennsylvania

Diane Lang
Montclair State University and Centenary College
Flanders, New Jersey

Nancy McGee
Macomb Community College
Warren, Michigan

Kate Maragliano
McGrath Library, Hilbert College
Hamburg, New York

Stephen Richmond
Art Institute of Phoenix
Phoenix, Arizona

Mary Gormandy White
Mobile Technical Institute
Mobile, Alabama

100% Information Literacy Success

CHAPTER OUTLINE

Workplace Requirements of Employees

Information Literacy: An Overview

Why Is Information Literacy Important?

Steps in Effective Research

1 Introduction to Information Literacy

THE BIG PICTURE

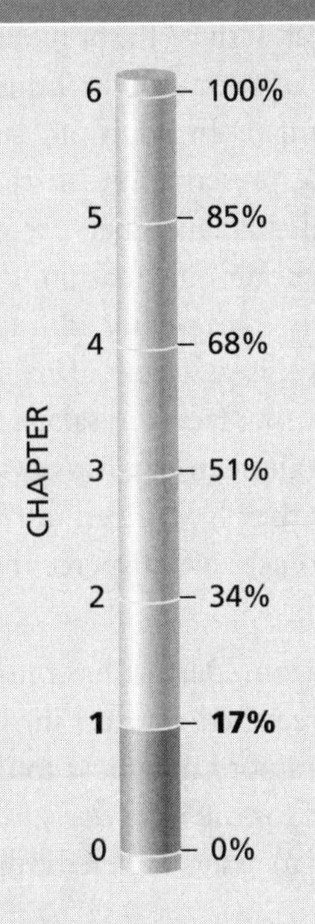

LEARNING OBJECTIVES

By the end of this chapter, students will achieve the following objectives:

- Define *information literacy*.
- List the specific skills required for an individual to be an information-literate student or professional.
- Explain the importance of knowing how to locate, access, retrieve, evaluate, use, and effectively communicate information in school and in the workplace.
- Explain the challenges facing an individual who does not possess information skills in school and in the workplace.

Information literacy is essential for success in any workplace situation.

1

CHAPTER 1 SCENARIO

Workplace requirements include the ability to find, evaluate, organize, and communicate information. Consider the following scenario, which illustrates the importance of information literacy skills in the workplace.

Derrick Washington just graduated from college with an associate degree in nursing and was hired at a long-term nursing facility as a caregiver. This facility has the philosophy that true patient care stems from a genuine concern for each individual patient and in-depth knowledge about the individual diseases and disorders challenging each patient. In light of this philosophy, the administration asks all staff members, regardless of position, to attend weekly inservice training sessions to learn more about the care of their patients. The staff members take turns presenting information about selected diseases, disorders, and other healthcare issues, including healthcare ethics, legal issues, economic issues, related community issues, aging issues, communication topics, and diversity topics.

Each staff member is assigned a topic and is asked to fully research the subject, select the most relevant information for the staff as a whole, develop a 1-to-2-page information sheet with a "Resources for Additional Learning" section, and create a "Tips for Patient Education" page for distribution to each staff member. In addition, staff members are required to deliver a 20-minute presentation on their topic to the entire group of care providers. All staff members are expected to participate, provide current and accurate information, and use excellent professional communication skills. The facility administration considers these inservice training sessions as essential to the facility's continued excellence and as a contributing factor in salary increases and promotions. Accordingly, each staff member is assessed quarterly on the effectiveness of the inservices they have given during the quarter. All staff members are expected to achieve 80 percent or better on these assessments.

Through self-reflection and honest evaluation, Derrick has found that he does not have the information skills required to excel in this workplace expectation. He realizes that he does not know how to determine what kind of information he will need for the inservices, how to find current information efficiently, or how to assess the credibility of information. In addition, he does not feel confident in his ability to organize the information effectively into a brief written summary or to make a professional presentation, even though he took related courses for these skills in school. He is significantly stressed about this employment requirement.

Imagine yourself to be in Derrick's position. Thoughtfully and honestly answer the following questions:

- How well do you think you could determine the kind and extent of information you might be asked to find so you are able to accomplish a professional task?
- How efficient would you be at finding the information in a library or on the Internet?
- How skilled are you at pulling significant points from a large body of information and organizing them into a 1–2 page summary for review by professionals in your field?
- How effectively could you make a presentation that would both engage and teach your colleagues?

WORKPLACE REQUIREMENTS OF EMPLOYEES

In 1990 the U.S. Department of Labor initiated a study to investigate and document the demands of the changing U.S. workplace and determine how successfully our parents, educational institutions, and workplaces were preparing individuals to compete. The resulting commission, the Secretary's Commission on Achieving Necessary Skills (SCANS), published the SCANS report. The results are summarized in Figure 1-1.

The SCANS report suggests that if parents and educational institutions help students develop the skills indicated in the report before graduating from high school, students will have better employment opportunities as adults. Also, employers must organize their businesses and hire employees with the same skills or face business failure locally, nationally, and in global competition. Finally, educational institutions at the primary, secondary, and post-secondary levels must teach and reinforce the recommended skills to prepare students to be

Workplace Know-How

The know-how identified by SCANS is made up of five competencies and a three-part foundation of skills and personal qualities that are needed for solid job performance. These include:

Competencies: Effective workers can productively use:

- **Resources**—allocating time, money, materials, space, and staff;
- **Interpersonal Skills**—working on teams, teaching others, serving customers, leading, negotiating, and working well with people from culturally diverse backgrounds;
- **Information**—acquiring and evaluating data, organizing and maintaining files, interpreting and communicating, and using computers to process information;
- **Systems**—understanding social, organizational, and technological systems, monitoring and correcting performance, and designing or improving systems;
- **Technology**—selecting equipment and tools, applying technology to specific tasks, and maintaining and troubleshooting technologies.

Foundation competence requires:

- **Basic Skills**—reading, writing, arithmetic and mathematics, speaking, and listening;
- **Thinking Skills**—thinking creatively, making decisions, solving problems, seeing things in the mind's eye, knowing how to learn, and reasoning;
- **Personal Qualities**—individual responsibility, self-esteem, sociability, self-management, and integrity.

Source: *SCANS Report for Workplace Know-How* (Washington, DC: U.S. Department of Labor, 1991).

Figure 1-1 SCANS Report

The SCANS report outlines competencies, skills, and personal qualities viewed as important for job success.

successful in the workplace or face the prospect of failing students, the community, and the nation as a whole.

Since the SCANS report was published, colleges and universities, state curriculum committees, the American Library Association, and numerous businesses and corporations have focused on defining, developing, and refining these required skill sets in more depth. Notice that a majority of the required skills for the workforce revolve around communication, information, and technology.

The end of the twentieth century has been referred to as the *dawn of the Information Age*, which is marked by significant "increased production of, communication of, consumption of, and reliance on information" (Berkman Center for Internet and Society at Harvard Law School, n.d.). With this definition in mind, information clearly is a key ingredient and the abilities to find, access, retrieve, evaluate, use, and communicate information are skills critical for workplace success. These skills are the foundation of **information literacy.**

INFORMATION LITERACY: AN OVERVIEW

1

According to the American Library Association (ALA), an information-literate person is "able to recognize when information is needed and has the ability to locate, evaluate, and use the information effectively" (ALA, 2005). To execute these information-related tasks effectively, students and professionals must develop an efficient information-gathering process and enhance specific information-related skills. Accordingly, the ALA has published information literacy standards for students in higher education (ALA, 2005).

Summarized, an information-literate individual should be able to complete the following information-related tasks. Each of these tasks reflects numerous skill sets, which are the focus of the next several chapters of this text.

- **DEFINE:** *Define the need, problem, or question.*

  For example, a small training company wants to start offering its training workshops to customers in another state. To do so legally, efficiently, and wisely, the company first must answer several questions about the new area: (1) Does the new state have any laws or regulations for this type of business? (2) Does the new area have competition that would make the decision to expand unwise? (3) Does the new area have enough potential customers—those who would be interested in the type of training the company offers—to make the training cost-effective? These are examples of the many questions that should be asked.
- **FIND:** *Locate, access, and retrieve the information from a variety of print, electronic, and human information sources.*

In the example, the company must find the information to answer the questions about expansion into the new state. The training manager responsible for the expansion must understand the specific resources that are available and that will provide her with the correct and current information. She then must be able to locate the resources and access the information.

Once she has accessed the information, she must be able to retrieve it so she can organize it and present it to the company president later. The information she needs might include state and local regulations, market reports, and demographic information. Sources might include state and local governments, market surveys, directories, and other data services. From numerous resources, the training manager must select the information that best serves the purpose.

- **EVALUATE:** *Assess the credibility, currency, reliability, validity, and appropriateness of the information retrieved.*

  Before the training manager actually uses the information, she must ensure that it is credible, current, reliable, and valid. For example, an information resource that provides market data from 1985 is not useful. Likewise, information published by a competing company may be biased. Credible resources must be used as a basis for making good business decisions.

- **ORGANIZE:** *Compile the information so it can be used to meet the information need, solve the problem, or answer the question.*

  Once the training manager has gathered all of the needed information, she must organize it so it can be used to answer her specific questions. For example, she might want to show trends in population, the influx of new companies that require her training, and specific data showing that her training has little competition. Organizing the information according to each question will allow her to prepare her presentation more effectively.

- **COMMUNICATE:** *Communicate the information legally and ethically using a variety of channels directed at a range of audiences.*

  Finally, the training manager must communicate the information to the president and other decision makers in the company. She has been asked to make a formal presentation to a board of directors and will use charts, graphs, and other visual representations of the data. She also has been asked to write a formal proposal and will have to provide accurate information about her information sources. The training manager's ability to present the information clearly, using professional language, will be vital to her success. She must cite her sources accurately and present her references in a way that gives appropriate credit to her information sources.

Information literacy assumes several professional skills that are important to every successful student and professional. These skills, sometimes referred to as *transferable skills* or *generic skills,* are the abilities important for career success, regardless of industry or job title. Critical thinking, creative thinking, problem solving, higher-order thinking, effective communication, and organization provide a foundation for information literacy.

CRITICAL THINKING

By definition, **critical thinking** employs skills that contribute to information literacy. Critical thinking and information literacy both require making a distinction between assumption and fact, suspending personal opinion and bias in favor of objectivity, and considering issues from multiple perspectives and in adequate depth. To achieve these objectives, you must think actively and systematically about information using a variety of strategies. Figure 1-2 illustrates only a few of the important critical thinking strategies. Critical thinking is more

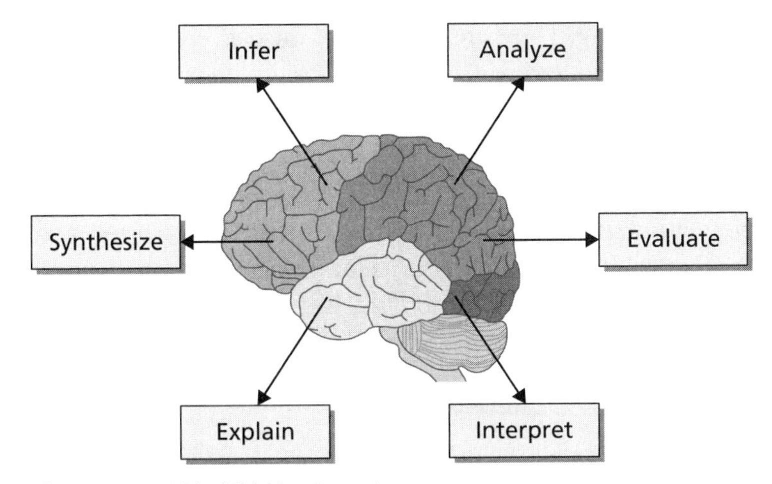

Figure 1-2 Critical Thinking Strategies
Critical thinking strategies can be categorized into six major areas.

than just thinking, which can sometimes be biased, uninformed, distorted, superficial, or incomplete. Critical thinking is necessary for effective use of information.

The following processes involved in critical thinking are illustrations from the training company expansion scenario in the previous section.

- **INFER:** *To draw conclusions from evidence or facts.*

  In the training company expansion scenario, the training manager responsible for the expansion inferred, from the lack of any significant training companies in the business directories she viewed, that her training company would have a good chance of being successful in the new state.

- **ANALYZE:** *To break down complex concepts into parts and then study how the parts are related to each other in making up the whole.*

  In the training company expansion scenario, the training manager had to analyze the various data she found. For example, from all of the companies doing business in the new area, she had to pull out those that might use her training. Her analysis involved multiple factors, including assessing the needs of companies and their ability to fund the training. She had to consider the perspectives of the decision makers in the companies as well as the perspective of her own organization. She also had to find out how many other companies provide the same type of training. These are examples of the data analysis needed to make a good decision.
- **EVALUATE:** *To examine critically given a specific set of criteria.*

  After broadly analyzing the training situation, the training manager had to critically examine the specific data, such as population statistics, marketing data, financial information, and the human resource requirements for the new training. In addition, to ensure an effective job, she had to evaluate her performance on each of the steps.
- **INTERPRET:** *To comprehend the meaning or significance of something.*

  In the training company expansion scenario, the training manager had to interpret the significance of the influx of new businesses into the state and relate this influx to the existing training options in the area. She also had to interpret the significance of the online training options and how these options were meeting the actual needs of the businesses. She had to consider the meaning of her analysis in light of these additional factors.

- **EXPLAIN:** *To make clear the thought process, facts, or concepts.*
  The training manager had to clearly explain and illustrate her recommendation to expand the company's training to the new state. She had to show how she arrived at the decision by presenting accurate, thorough, and effectively organized data.
- **SYNTHESIZE:** *To combine separate thoughts to form a concept.*
  Finally, to make a sound recommendation, the training manager had to take all of the information, including the recommendations of her subordinates, the state agency representatives she talked with, and potential customers, and combine this information with the empirical data (facts and figures) she obtained in her research

CREATIVE THINKING

Creative thinking is the process of actively exploring possibilities, generating alternatives, keeping an open mind toward change, and combining ideas to create something new or to view old concepts in new ways. The common phrase "think outside the box" refers to thinking creatively. Effective creative thinking is innovative, yet takes into consideration facts and realistic constraints. Creative thinkers use their imagination, are highly expressive, and are not restricted by existing ideas or barriers. They seek and embrace support from others to gain different perspectives.

For example, a construction foreman faced with increasing safety at the jobsite might hand out safety pamphlets and ask each laborer to read the information. A more creative solution, though, might be to create performance competition among three different teams by giving a safety quiz identifying safety issues on the jobsite, and by rewarding the team that accrues the most points over the life of the project. Or the foreman might seek input from others to see what safety programs have been effective in the past.

Effective information users combine critical thinking and creative thinking in their approach to an information need or problem-solving situation.

PROBLEM SOLVING

Problem solving entails a systematic process to find a solution to a question or issue. Being information-literate includes knowing how to analyze and apply information to solve problems successfully. Steps in the problem solving process consist of: (1) defining the problem, (2) looking for possible causes of the problem, (3) developing possible solutions for the problem, (4) evaluating each possible solution to determine the best one, (5) implementing the best solution, and (6) evaluating the results. Figure 1-3 illustrates a simplified version of this process.

- **DEFINE THE PROBLEM.** *A problem must be well understood before it can be solved. To define a problem, use information to answer the questions: Who? What? Where? When? How? Why? How much?*

  As an example, consider an office network situation in which the process of backing up the information on the office network is inefficient and is taking too long. In this situation, the problem first must be defined by thoroughly by reviewing the facts, and assessing the processes used by the office manager who is responsible for the biweekly backups. Many of the files

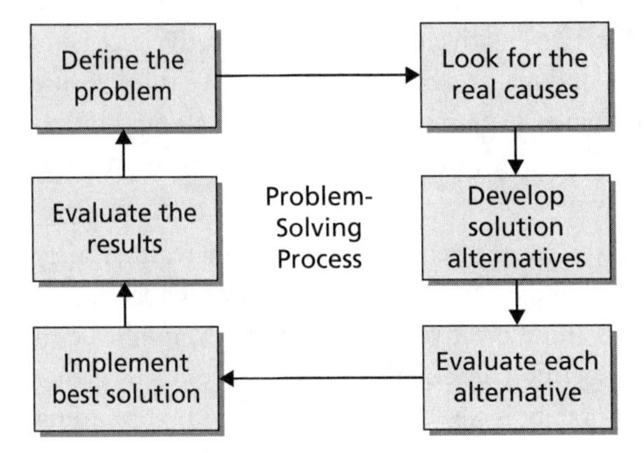

Figure 1-3 The Problem-Solving Process
Effective problem solving involves six major steps.

are crucial and contain information that, if lost, would cost the company money and time.

In the current backup system, the office manager burns the latest files to CD-ROMs and takes the CD-ROMs home to store the backups offsite for safekeeping. The problem is that this process is too time-consuming, the CD-ROMs are not as reliable as other data-storage options over a long time, and the offsite storage is not secure.

- **LOOK FOR THE REAL CAUSES.** *Ensure that you know the exact cause(s) of the problem and that you understand these causes thoroughly. With only a superficial study of the situation, real causes of a problem may be hidden, so careful analysis and the consideration of multiple perspectives are important.*

  In the data-storage scenario, a closer look at this situation reveals that the office manager is not very knowledgeable about data backup and storage, and that burning CD-ROMs is the only method he knows. At least part of the real cause of the problem is a lack of skill on the part of the person responsible for the network and data.

- **DEVELOP SOLUTION ALTERNATIVES.** *Because getting input from appropriate people contributes to developing possible solutions, engage others in brainstorming as part of the creative thinking process to generate as many alternatives as possible.*

  Among several potential options for solving the data backup and storage dilemma are these: (1) The office manager could continue to use the CD-ROMs as the backup and data-storage method; (2) the company could purchase a tape backup for data storage; (3) instead of CD-ROMs, the office manager could burn DVDs, which hold much more information; (4) the company could purchase an external hard drive for backup and then store the hard drive offsite; and (5) the company could use an offsite data backup and storage system offered by a third party. An issue related to both the problem and the solution is the need to provide the office manager with training on data backup and storage.

- **EVALUATE EACH ALTERNATIVE.** *Consider each alternative to determine which solution or combination of solutions works best.*

1

Getting an outside opinion from a neutral party contributes another perspective and additional data to the evaluation.

In the data backup and storage scenario, each alternative should be evaluated using a set of predetermined criteria. Because the criteria and the questions asked vary with each situation, knowing the kind of information needed is necessary to define the relevant questions. In this case, the following questions are important: (1) How much does each system cost? (2) How reliable is each system, and how long does each system last? (3) How difficult is each system to implement and maintain? (4) How long does the actual backup process take? (5) How secure is each system? (6) What is the process for data recovery?

- **IMPLEMENT THE BEST SOLUTION.** *After selecting the best solution, implement it carefully.*

  In the data backup and storage scenario, the company has chosen the solution of contracting with a third party for offsite data backup and storage. Research revealed a relatively low cost, a high level of security and reliability, ease of implementation, and quick recovery of data, if needed. The company signed on with a reliable data backup and storage company and implemented the process within a few days. Also, the office manager received free training on how to use the new system from that company. He also learned how to increase the security and organization of the company's data and file system.

- **EVALUATE THE RESULTS.** *Finally, assess whether the solution worked. Is the problem solved? If not, do further evaluation to determine what worked, what did not, and what changes are appropriate. Assess whether information was adequate, whether it was used effectively, and whether the way the information was communicated influenced the outcome in any way. After any changes have been implemented, repeat the cycle.*

  In the data backup and storage scenario, the company compared the results with the old system, assessed the overall security, and reviewed the existing data-management system. It was determined that, although the service did incur a monthly expense, the extra cost was offset by increased security and the officer manager's increased efficiency. The company also decided to revisit the problem in one month to ensure that the data indeed were being backed up as planned, and stored appropriately.

HIGHER-ORDER THINKING

Higher-order thinking is described in detail in Bloom's taxonomy (Bloom, 1956), which suggests six levels of thinking, beginning with the lowest level (Knowledge) and increasing to the highest level (Evaluation). Each level describes a different way to think about information. The lowest level is superficial, considering straightforward facts. An example of this level is being able to name the states and their capitals. The highest level reflects deep, complex thinking, in which information is judged critically to reach a decision. The training company manager's process is an example of using the higher levels of Bloom's taxonomy. The diagram in Figure 1-4 illustrates Bloom's taxonomy with its six levels of thinking about information. An information-literate individual will use all levels of thinking at various times, depending on the information need and the goal he or she is trying to achieve. Academic and professional activities tend to require the higher levels of thinking more often.

The following action verbs represent strategies for thinking effectively at each level of Bloom's taxonomy.

- *Knowledge:* Define, identify, describe, recognize, label, list, match, name, reproduce, outline, recall, reproduce
- *Comprehension:* Explain, generalize, extend, comprehend, give examples, summarize, translate, paraphrase, rewrite, predict

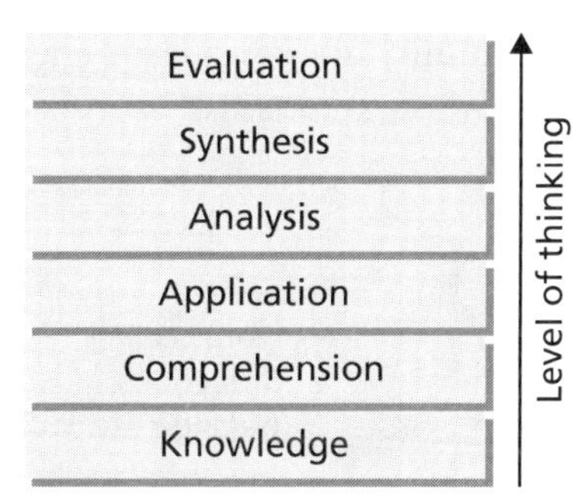

Figure 1-4 Bloom's Taxonomy

The six levels in Bloom's higher-order thinking taxonomy begin with broad, basic thinking (knowledge) and end with more advanced, complex thinking (evaluation).

1

- *Application:* Apply, compute, change, construct, develop, manipulate, solve, show, illustrate, produce, relate, use, operate, discover, modify
- *Analysis:* Analyze, break down, infer, separate, diagram, differentiate, contrast, compare
- *Synthesis:* Categorize, generate, design, devise, compile, rearrange, reorganize, revise, reconstruct, combine, write, tell
- *Evaluation:* Conclude, defend, critique, discriminate, judge, interpret, justify, support

Note that the level of thinking complexity increases as you move from basic knowledge to evaluation.

EFFECTIVE COMMUNICATION

Successful students and professionals must be able to communicate information effectively to many different types of audiences and in a variety of situations. For effective communication to happen, the sender of a message should understand the basic communication process shown in Figure 1-5.

The context in which a communication occurs influences the way information and messages are used, expressed, and received. For example, your communication style in a group of friends is likely to differ from the communication style you use with a group of your professors. The concept of *discourse communities* refers to different groups and the unique rules and standards (formal and informal) of each group for communicating. Effective communication takes place when the standards of a specific discourse community are considered and information is communicated according to those standards.

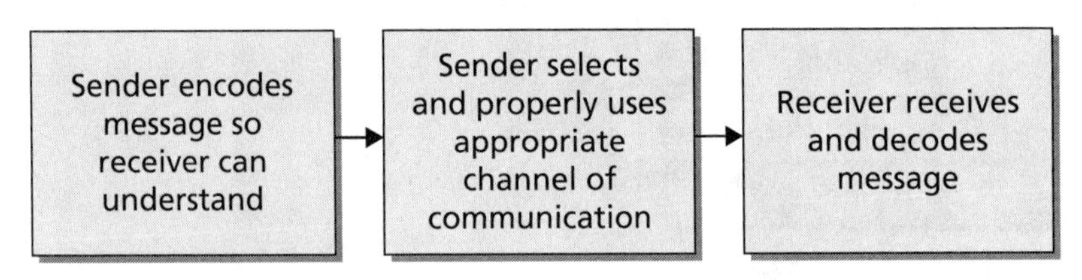

Figure 1-5 The Communication Process

The communication process involves a sender who encodes a message and then selects and utilizes an appropriate channel so a receiver can receive and decode the message.

The standards include aspects of communication such as level of formality, language, and style guidelines. For example, communication with your professors (one discourse community) will be more effective when you observe standards of professionalism and appropriate formality. Conversely, your friends (another discourse community) would find you stuffy and overly formal if you were to use the same communication style with them. Messages are sent and received effectively when the conventions of a discourse community are observed. (Trupe, 2001; Rice Online Writing Lab, n.d.)

A look at a brief scenario illustrates discourse communities and the basic communication process. Dr. Stewart has just received the results from a series of blood tests for his patient, John, who is suffering from extreme fatigue. Dr. Stewart has to tell John that he has hypoglycemia, a severely lowered blood glucose (blood sugar) level. First, Dr. Stewart must consider the discourse community. He is communicating with a member of the patient community (versus the medical community), so he must encode the message into a form that the receiver (John) can understand. Because John is not at all familiar with technical medical terms, Dr. Stewart must use simple, layperson terms so John can clearly understand the details of his condition.

Next, Dr. Stewart must select and properly use a medium or channel to send this message. With confidential medical information, Dr. Stewart decides not to leave a message on John's answering machine but, instead, decides to meet with John in person so Dr. Stewart can answer any questions and help John initiate the steps to manage his hypoglycemia. Dr. Stewart also decides to use as a visual aid an anatomical illustration of the digestive system and blood pathway to help John understand the importance of eating regular meals. Finally, John must actually receive this information and decode it accurately so he will understand his medical condition.

Dr. Stewart has selected illustrations and explanations that are understandable to a member of the patient community. Consider how this might be different if Dr. Stewart were providing this information to a member of the medical community.

If any part of the communication process is missing or misunderstood, the message will not be communicated as intended. Accordingly, an effective communicator must develop specific skills related to each step in the communication process and be able to select the most effective approach based on the situation.

To encode and send a message successfully, the communicator must develop the abilities to

- write well
- speak in public
- interact effectively with others
- use visual elements in communicating an idea
- use a variety of technologies (telephone, computer, e-mail, other Internet communication tools, scanners and cameras, audio and video recorders, etc.) to send the message.

A careful study of this process reveals that the sender is responsible for ensuring that the message is received as intended. The receiver also plays a role in the communication process by asking clarifying questions and actively participating in the discourse.

CRITICAL THINKING QUESTIONS

1. If a workplace professional were said to be computer-literate, how would you describe his or her skills specifically?
2. Assuming you are not the librarian but are said to be a great researcher and literate in using the library, what kind of skills do you think you would have?
3. To be media-literate, what specific workplace or school situations might you need? What specific skills would you have?
4. Think about the careers that intrigue you and that you might see yourself working in. How might you have to be visually literate? How would this help you communicate or achieve some other workplace or school goal?
5. What skills do you think are essential for someone who is technology-literate? Do these skills differ in different career areas?

ORGANIZATION

A person who is organized has a systematic way to group information, take notes on research so the main points can be identified, categorize material so the information is easily found, and log steps and resources for later reference. An information-literate individual must understand how to use a variety of organizational strategies to gather information and communicate it effectively. Specific skills include understanding and logically using electronic and print file management systems, practicing time-management techniques, breaking down complex tasks to manageable objectives, and appropriately using a variety of graphic organizers such as Venn diagrams, flowcharts, tables, Gantt charts, organizational charts, concept maps, and so forth. Each of these tools will be described later in the text.

Information literacy is an umbrella term that encompasses several types of literacy. An information-literate individual recognizes that all types of literacy are important and strives to become proficient in the skill sets required for each. These skill sets often overlap and support each other, and all rely on the transferable skills described earlier. The following types of literacy and their associated skills are important components of information literacy.

Hardware

Software

Internet

Multimedia

File management

Security

Figure 1-6 Computer Literacy Competencies

Computer literacy involves knowledge and skills in six major areas related to computers.

COMPUTER LITERACY

Computer literacy involves a basic understanding of how a computer works and how it can be used to complete a task. A computer-literate individual understands the various terms associated with computer hardware, as well as common computer software applications. Figure 1-6 illustrates the various competency areas that make up computer literacy.

LIBRARY LITERACY

Library literacy encompasses an understanding of the different kinds of information resources housed in a library—books, encyclopedias, reference materials, directories, catalogs, indexes, databases, periodicals, visual resources, audio resources, graphic resources, and so forth. Library literacy also includes knowing how to locate the resources in the library physically or electronically, understanding how to find and access information within each resource, being knowledgeable about correct referencing processes, and being able to get help from a librarian when necessary. Today, many libraries use both print and electronic resources and search tools. An important aspect of library literacy is to know which technology is most appropriate for the task.

©BananaStock Ltd.

Books and periodicals

Databases and directories

Catalogs and indexes

Media resources

Reference materials

Figure 1-7 Knowledge Areas of Library Literacy
Library literacy involves knowledge and skills in five major areas.

Figure 1-7 illustrates only a few of the many knowledge areas required for library literacy.

MEDIA LITERACY

One definition of **media literacy** is "the ability to decode, analyze, evaluate, and produce communication in a variety of forms" (Trent Think Tank on Media Literacy, 1989). In many cases, print form (print media) is appropriate and sufficient. At other times, audio, visual, graphic, web-based, interactive, electronic, and other forms are better media for the communication. The information-literate individual must understand the many options available and know how to translate the information into the best choice. Media-literate individuals also understand the advantages, disadvantages, challenges, and purposes of each type of media.

A component of media literacy is visual literacy, "the ability, through knowledge of the basic visual elements, to understand the meaning and components of the image" (On-line Visual Literacy Project, 1998). Though information-literate individuals do not have to be graphic designers or accomplished artists, in many cases visual elements are the best choice for conveying a message. Information-literate individuals must understand how to find, create, format, alter, and embed visual elements into the message, using basic computer software and other tools.

TECHNOLOGY LITERACY

Finally, the information-literate individual must be able to use a variety of technologies to find and access information, as well as to effectively organize, use, and communicate information. These skills make up **technology literacy**. Included in these technology skills are the ability to use basic computer software programs (e.g., word-processing, spreadsheets, presentation tools, databases), the Internet, and supporting tools such as search engines, file-management systems, and so forth. And, because technology changes quickly, information-literate individuals must update their technology skills continuously to stay current and be able to use their existing skills in new ways.

Information literacy is not just for the technical student or the business and technology professional. Information skills are required in every career, and this trend can be expected to grow. For example, the health professions (which at one time were considered "nontechnical") are using technology for managing patient records, charting patient progress, and operating equipment. All professionals rely on some type of information to complete their job tasks successfully. To be successful in a career, the college graduate no longer can rely solely on the information learned in school. Information is constantly changing.

Today, the professional must acquire new knowledge and skills continuously. For example, an allied health professional will have to keep up with new procedures, medication, diseases, and treatments. A construction professional must keep up with new materials, codes, and techniques. A business professional must be able to gather data on markets, the competition, and new avenues for products and services. New ideas, technologies, processes, discoveries, and information are constantly being added to the body of knowledge in every field. To lack information literacy is to be significantly hindered in job success and advancement.

This chapter provides only a general overview of skills that are important in information literacy, a "big picture" outline of the many

Reflection Question

1. Review the following quote: "In this knowledge-oriented workplace, information literacy is the key to power." What does this mean to you in your own career path? Write down some specific examples of how this might be true for you.

considerations that are important to you as a college student and as professional advancing through your career. The remaining chapters will provide more detailed strategies and information about these areas.

WHY IS INFORMATION LITERACY IMPORTANT?

Homes, schools, libraries, and workplaces are becoming increasingly outfitted with advanced technology including powerful computers, high-speed Internet connections, sophisticated software applications, convenient searching tools, and numerous media devices such as digital cameras, scanners, computer fax machines, and wireless devices. We know the technology is available, but do we know how to harness this technology to solve our problems and answer our questions? What do we do when we are faced with so much information? How will we know that what we find is credible? How will we communicate this information to all the people who need to know? How do we even know what questions to ask to begin to solve our information problems?

Without advanced knowledge and skills, students and professionals alike are at a significant disadvantage in their work environments. Problems facing individuals who lack information skills include

- asking the wrong questions (and consequently getting the wrong answers!)
- using limited or inappropriate sources of information
- using inaccurate or misleading information
- accessing outdated information
- finding incomplete information
- using biased or one-sided resources
- being inefficient in research and wasting time
- being disorganized
- communicating the information ineffectively

We cannot just be excellent learners. We must be lifelong learners to keep pace with advancing technology and new information. A

Reflection Questions

1. Reflect on your area of study and the job-related tasks in your current or future career. What sources and information will you need to be able to locate, access, retrieve, and use information? Try to list as many different areas and types of information as you can. Expand this list as you think of additional types of information and sources.
2. How do you think you might be asked to communicate new information in your workplace? List as many different ways or formats as you can. Be specific.
3. Imagine yourself in the role of manager or owner of a company, organization, or facility similar to the kind in which you want to work during your career. Relative to information literacy, what information skills would you want your new employees to have? Why? How would you, as the owner/manager, be at a disadvantage if your employees were information-illiterate? (Think about this question as you compare your facility to a competing facility with highly skilled employees in information areas.)

college graduate's first job represents only the first steps. Career advancement requires continuous development of knowledge and skills, as well as the ability and willingness to adapt quickly to the constantly changing tools of the industry. Career advancement in today's information world requires well-developed information skills. Lifelong learning requires lifelong students to take the initiative to continue to learn and also to figure out what they need to learn.

STEPS IN EFFECTIVE RESEARCH

Successfully using information to meet a need can be defined in the series of steps illustrated in Figure 1-8. The remainder of this text discusses each step in detail and explores the required information skills.

STEP 1: DEFINE THE NEED

Before you can even begin to seek the proper information, you must establish and articulate the need for that information. This requires consulting with appropriate individuals to communicate and define the need. A need can be a problem that must be solved, a question that must be answered, or a task that must be performed. For example, an instructor may assign to students the task of writing an essay on a controversial issue. In this case, information is needed to describe each side of the issue in depth. The student also must be able to communicate

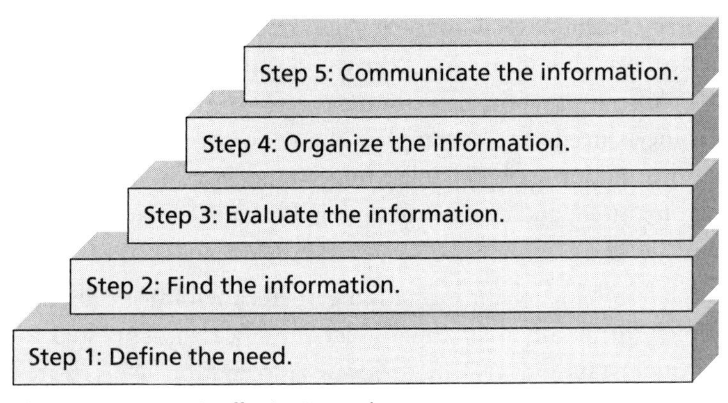

Figure 1-8 Steps in Effective Research
There are five steps to effective research.

REFLECTION QUESTIONS

1. Think carefully about your career field or a field in which you might be interested. What technologies do you predict for this field in the next ten years? How do you see a job in this field changing because of these technologies? Write down as many different ideas as you can.
2. How might you prepare yourself for continued success and career advancement in a specific field? What about the workplace in general?

CRITICAL THINKING QUESTIONS

1. An obsolete employee is one who no longer has the skills required to do the job. What specifically might an obsolete employee in your career field look like in ten years?
2. How do ambitious employees prevent themselves from becoming obsolete? Be specific, and relate your ideas specifically to your field of study.

the information in the required format. In the workplace, a departmental team may be asked to solve a production problem. In this case, the information need is to find information about potential technology solutions and then to evaluate which solution is the best option in light of the company's financial and time constraints. Finally, the team must communicate this solution to decision makers.

questions to ask 

- What kind of information do I need? (facts, figures, statistics, opinions, sides of an issue, historical/background, profile, interview, primary, secondary, etc.)
- How much information do I need? (limited scope, in-depth coverage, summary or overview, etc.)
- What parameters should I follow? (time period, geographical location, age or gender, point of view, etc.)
- Who will be receiving this information? (practitioners, professionals, laypeople, scientists, team members, colleagues, clients, patients, etc.)

STEP 2: FIND THE INFORMATION

Step 2 involves creating a research strategy customized to the task at hand. A research strategy is a kind of map used to avoid wasting time and wandering aimlessly through the massive amounts of information available in libraries, on the Internet, and in other locations. A research strategy includes deciding what resources to use, whether the resources are available and cost-effective, if using specific resources provides significant benefit, how the resources can be accessed, and what timeline is needed to accomplish the research. To develop this map, the information gatherer must understand how information is produced, organized, and communicated, in both formal and informal situations.

With plan in hand, the information gatherer then must call upon a variety of information skills to conduct the research. This step assumes an understanding of how to locate information using search tools and information-retrieval systems, how to use appropriate investigative methods to obtain the best information, how to find the information within a given resource, how to take useful notes, and how to extract information and save it in an organized manner.

questions to ask

- What information sources should I use? (encyclopedias, professional journals, people, directories, databases, popular magazines, maps, videos, etc.)
- Where do I find these resources? (library, Internet, individuals, companies, government resources, librarian, etc.)
- How do I search for the information within each resource? (index, electronic search engine, card catalog, etc.)
- How should I retrieve the information once I find it? (download, photocopy, interlibrary loan, print, etc.)
- How do I manage the information that I retrieve? (electronic files, print file folders, etc.)

STEP 3: EVALUATE THE INFORMATION

Evaluating the research results requires the information gatherer to apply a set of criteria to determine if the information is reliable, valid, accurate, current, and free from bias. In this part of the evaluation the credibility of the actual information sources is assessed. Information also must be evaluated to determine if it meets the research need. This type of evaluation requires filtering, from all of the collected data, information that is important to the original question or problem.

questions to ask

- Is the information current?
- Is the information credible?
- Is the information accurate?
- Is the information relevant to the need?
- Is the information useful?
- Is the information free from bias?

In the next chapters we will define more extensively what is involved in answering each of these questions.

STEP 4: ORGANIZE THE INFORMATION

An information-literate individual uses systematic strategies to organize information so it can be communicated in the most effective way. Organization starts with managing the information retrieved in the research process. For many research projects, a large amount of information is available, some of which may not be useful or directly related to the need. Sometimes it is difficult to know if all of the information is important until the information gathering is complete. Keeping information organized as it is collected simplifies the evaluation process. Information also must be organized to achieve the communication goal. Information can be organized and presented according to several criteria, which will be discussed in depth in chapter 5.

questions to ask

- How do I organize the information so I can find main ideas, key issues, different viewpoints, etc.?
- How can I think about the information in new ways?
- How do I manage a large amount of information?
- How do I organize the information so it is presented logically and appropriately? (chronologically, priority of elements, problem/solution, deductive order, inductive order, etc.)

STEP 5: COMMUNICATE THE INFORMATION

The information-literate individual must communicate the information to others effectively so it can be used to solve the problem, answer the question, or meet the original need. Effective communication considers many factors and can be transmitted through a variety of channels: written documents, verbal presentations, visual presentations, and a variety of electronic formats. The communication also must be legal and ethical according to copyright laws, intellectual property standards, and the accurate citation of information sources.

questions to ask

- Who is my audience? Am I communicating on a casual topic or for business? Is the setting formal or relaxed? The type of audience and the setting will determine how you will deliver your information.
- What channel should be used to communicate the research results? (written, verbal, visual, electronic, etc.)
- For the selected channel, what specific format best meets the communication need? (proposal, narrative, research report, slide presentation, image, diagram, etc.)
- How do I properly reference the resources I use and give appropriate credit to the original authors of the information?

Finally, the entire research process and results should be evaluated to determine if the information has met the need sufficiently, solved the problem, or answered the original questions. If not, the process should be evaluated and changes made if appropriate.

Each of the next five chapters in this text will address one of the steps in the research process and explain the specific skills that an information-literate professional needs.

success steps

STEPS IN EFFECTIVE RESEARCH

Step 1: Define the need.

Step 2: Find the information.

Step 3: Evaluate the information.

Step 4: Organize the information.

Step 5: Communicate the information.

In the scenario presented at the beginning of this chapter, Derrick Washington had the goal of succeeding in his new position and advancing quickly by accomplishing the expected tasks. He determined that to accomplish this goal, he must fully develop many different skills related to information and the research process. He also realized that lifelong learning would be essential to lifelong success.

REFLECTION QUESTIONS

1. Which steps in the research process do you think you currently do well?
2. In which steps do you think you need to develop more knowledge and skill?
3. What do you think are the most difficult steps for you to complete? Why?
4. What do you think are the easiest steps to complete? Why?

learning activities

Activity #1: Self-Analysis: Research Process

Goal: To reflect critically on your current process for finding and using information and to generate a list of areas for improvement

Think carefully and write down your answers to each of the following questions:

1. When you are given a research task, what typically is your first step? Then what do you do? Sketch your personal and realistic research process from beginning to end.
2. What resources do you typically use to find information? List each resource you have used in recent years (e.g., encyclopedia, dictionary, journal, newspaper, directory, website).
3. What resources do you commonly use in a library?
4. What online resources do you commonly use for research?
5. What search tools are you proficient at using (printed and/or electronic)?
6. How specifically do you copy down and organize the information you find?

Rating Table

Area	Rating 1–5
Critical thinking	
Creative thinking	
Problem solving	
Higher-order thinking	
Effective communication	
Organization	
Computer literacy	
Library literacy	
Media literacy	
Visual literacy	
Technology literacy	
Effective research	

7. How do you organize your electronic files on your computer?
8. On a scale from 1 to 5 where 1 = need significant improvement and 5 = expert, rate yourself in the areas listed on the Rating Table. Be honest.

Activity #2: Predicting the Future of Information

***Goal:* To emphasize the importance of information literacy for the future**

STEP 1: As a group, brainstorm answers to the following questions. Use your imagination. Think critically and creatively. Remember that in brainstorming, the goal is to generate as many ideas as possible, but not to judge or evaluate these ideas.

- What will libraries look like in ten years? In twenty years?
- How will people communicate with each other in ten years? In twenty years?
- What will computers look like in ten years? What will they be able to do that they cannot do now? In twenty years?

STEP 2: Organize your list into descriptive categories and be prepared to compare your list with those of other groups in your class.

Activity #3: Web Research

***Goal:* To develop a full understanding of the importance of information literacy in career success**

STEP 1: Go to the website of the American Library Association (www.ala.org)

STEP 2: Once there, use the site's search tool to find the Information Literacy resources. Read the information provided.

STEP 3: Go to the Google search engine and complete a search using "information literacy" as the search term. Explore at least two additional websites related to information literacy. What are others doing in the area of information literacy, and how do they describe the various skill sets?

STEP 3: List at least twenty different specific skills you know that you need to personally develop related to finding, accessing, retrieving, evaluating, using, and communicating information. Be prepared to share your list with your classmates.

STEP 4: Place this list in your Learning Portfolio.

LEARNING OBJECTIVES REVISITED

Review the learning objectives for this chapter and rate your level of achievement for each objective, using the rating scale provided. For each objective on which you do not rate yourself as a 3, outline a plan of action that you will take to fully achieve the objective. Include a timeframe for this plan.

1 = did not achieve objective successfully
2 = understand what is needed but need more study or practice
3 = achieved learning objective thoroughly

	1	2	3
Define Information literacy.	☐	☐	☐
List the specific skills required for an individual to be an information-literate student or professional.	☐	☐	☐
Explain the importance of knowing how to locate, access, retrieve, evaluate, use, and effectively communicate information in school and in the workplace.	☐	☐	☐
Explain the challenges facing an individual who does not possess information skills in school and in the workplace.	☐	☐	☐

Steps to Achieve Unmet Objectives

Steps	Due Date
1. ______________________	__________
2. ______________________	__________
3. ______________________	__________
4. ______________________	__________

POTENTIAL ITEMS FOR LEARNING PORTFOLIO

Refer to the "Developing Portfolios" section at the front of this text for more information on learning portfolios. Consider adding the following results from this chapter's learning activities or even ideas of your own to your learning portfolio.

- List of 20 Information Skills You Know You Need to Develop

REFERENCES

American Library Association (2005). *Information Literacy competency standards for higher education.* Retrieved September 5, 2006 from http://www. ala.org/ala/acrl/acrlstandards/informationliteracycompetency.htm#ildef

Berkman Center for Internet and Society at Harvard Law School (n.d.). Glossary of terms. Retrieved September 5, 2006 from http://cyber.law.harvard.edu/readinessguide/glossary.html

Bloom B. S. (1956). *Taxonomy of educational objectives, Handbook I: The cognitive domain.* New York: David McKay.

On-Line Visual Literacy Project (1998). *What is visual literacy?* Retrieved September 5, 2006 from http://www.pomona.edu/Academics/courserelated/classprojects/Visual-lit/intro/intro.html

Rice Online Writing Lab (n.d.). *Understanding your discourse community.* Retrieved September 8, 2006 from http://www.ruf.rice.edu/~riceowl/understanding_your_discourse_community.htm

Trent Think Tank on Media Literacy, Ontario, Canada (1989). [Digital] Literacy: *Rethinking education and training in a digital world. What is media literacy?* Retrieved September 5, 2006 from http://digitalliteracy.mwg.org/studies.html

Trupe, A. L. (2001). *Effective writing text: Discourse communities.* Retrieved August 22, 2006 from http://www.bridgewater.edu/~atrupe/ENG101/Text/discom.htm

CHAPTER OUTLINE

The Research Process

Primary and Secondary Information Sources

Library Information Sources

Information Retrieval Systems

2 Determining the Information You Need

THE BIG PICTURE

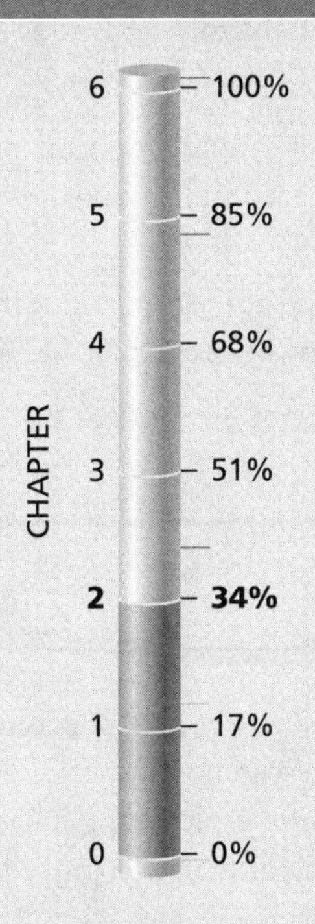

LEARNING OBJECTIVES

By the end of this chapter, students will achieve the following objectives:

- Explain the need for a main research question and relevant, focused research questions.
- Develop effective main research questions and focused research questions.
- Differentiate between primary and secondary information sources.
- Explain various ways to present information.
- Explain various ways to access information.
- Identify and describe common information sources.

Many jobs require research either on the Internet or in the library.

2

CHAPTER 2 SCENARIO

In every field, circumstances that require researching and applying information arise. Consider the following scenario as one example of the role and importance of research in the workplace.

Charley Murphy works as an assistant manager at a large electronics retail store. He realizes that to provide better customer service, he and his staff need to know much more than the average consumer about electronic equipment. Being able to answer any question that arises or know where to find the answers to questions will have a direct and positive impact on sales. Charley plans to assign a specific type of equipment—television, stereo, DVD and CD recorder/players, computers, printers and scanners, PDAs, cell phones, digital cameras, and other electronic equipment—to each member of his staff to research. Because he wants each member to provide some specific information, Charley realizes that he has to provide an example of the type of report he expects. To complete his report, he must do some research on the equipment. What does Charley need to know about researching the electronics industry so he can train his staff to better prepare the assigned reports?

Imagine yourself in Charley's place. Thoughtfully and honestly answer the following questions:

- How well do you think you could determine the kind and extent of the information you need to accomplish your information goal?
- How effective do you think you would be at creating a research question and focused questions to guide your research?
- What specific types of resources could you use to find the information you need?

REFLECTION QUESTIONS

Think of situations you have been in that require information on subjects you know nothing about.

1. What process did you use to learn more about the subject?
2. Did you have a plan?
3. What steps did you follow to find the information you needed?

THE RESEARCH PROCESS

On any given day, you consciously or subconsciously make decisions and solve problems. This involves a process. Research requires following a process to retrieve information on a specific topic, using reliable search tools to find the information, and being able to recognize the information as useful or irrelevant. Effective research employs the problem-solving skills discussed in chapter 1.

Review the steps in effective research presented in chapter 1. For now, our focus is on Step 1: Define the Need.

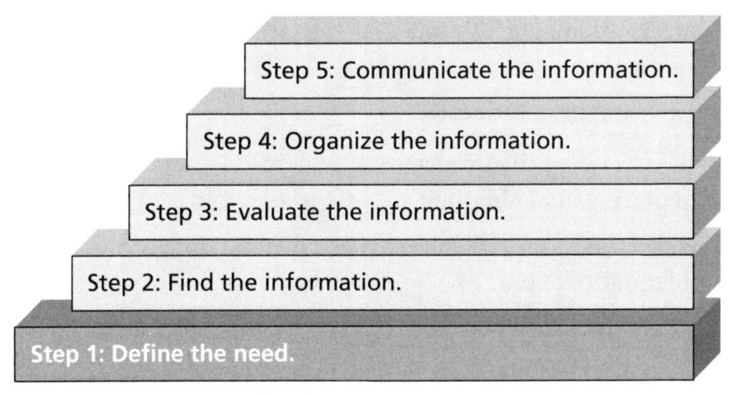

Research Process Step 1: Define the need

The first step of any research project should be to clearly define what is needed.

DEFINING A TOPIC

In school, your research topic most likely will be determined by its relevancy to the assignment. Your instructor may assign a specific topic or give you a range of topics from which to choose. Examples of other criteria for selecting topics are current events or current needs in a field, organizational goals and priorities, market trends, or training needs. These topics are more relevant to the workplace and represent research that you might do later in your career. The criteria for selecting a topic will depend largely on your field, organizational needs, and audience.

To be efficient, you first must clearly define the concepts related to your topic and the related information need. A need can be a problem that must be solved, a question that must be answered, or a task that must be performed. This need must be defined and communicated clearly. One way to define this need is to formulate a research question as a starting point for the research.

THE MAIN RESEARCH QUESTION

The main research question should include the key terms or concepts that are relevant to your topic. An effective research question will not be too broad or you will have too much information to sort through, and will not be so narrow that you are confined in your research. It should focus your research appropriately for your topic and your audience. Time and effort spent on developing an effective research question will save time and effort later in the research process.

Review the following examples of effective and ineffective research questions.

Effective research questions:

1. What effect does divorce have on academic achievement in elementary school children?
2. How did the Electoral College affect the outcome of the 2000 presidential election?
3. What are the differences between the various processors available for computers?

Ineffective research questions:

1. Who was Benjamin Franklin?
2. Should older people be allowed to drive?
3. Does the United States have a good foreign policy?

An effective research question poses a question that can be answered with verifiable facts. It is phrased in a way that avoids subjective responses or opinions. It is sufficiently specific to address the real need or purpose of the research. For example, effective research question #1 is specific. The answer to this question can be formed by searching library and other information resources to find verifiable facts. If no information is available, a study can be conducted to compare the academic performance of children from divorced parents with the academic performance of children from two-parent families. If the study is conducted properly using sound scientific investigative methods, the result should be useful information about how divorce affects academic performance in children.

By contrast, ineffective research question #1 (about Benjamin Franklin) is too broad to be useful in directing the research process. Benjamin Franklin's life has many facets. The best answer to this question depends on the purpose of the information. If you are collecting information on American statesmen, you would focus on the political life of Franklin. If you want information on inventors, you would describe Franklin by looking at his scientific endeavors. Perhaps your goal is a general biography about influential Americans. Your perspective would be different, and you would seek different kinds of information from different information sources. Until the question is narrowed, you cannot search effectively for information or conduct research. You also would organize the information differently depending on which aspect of Benjamin Franklin's life is selected.

Now look at ineffective research question #2. This question is also too vague to be effective and is phrased in a way that solicits opinion, not fact. For example, if you were to ask this question to a group of older people (or related information sources), you might get a very different answer than if you were to ask the question to a group of individuals who have had loved ones injured or killed by an older driver. And the question lacks a definition of "older" as well as criteria for assessment. The question is closed-ended, meaning that it is phrased in such a way that solicits a short, yes-or-no response.

Ineffective research question #3 also is vague, broad, and subjective. What aspect of foreign policy is in question? From whose perspective should the question be answered? What political party? What country? What is the purpose of the question? When questions such as these are necessary to understand the research question, it may be too general and broad. Answering these questions provides direction to your research project.

Opinion and judgment are different. Both are subjective in nature, in that both require your ideas and thoughts. Judgment, however, is supported by facts and verifiable data, whereas opinion is not. In college and in the workplace, you may be asked for your judgment on a topic or issue. An example in school is a position paper in which you are asked to state and support your stance on a topic. A workplace example is your being asked to provide a recommendation for a course of action. In both cases, you are being asked, in a sense, for your opinion. To be considered a reliable researcher, you must use relevant facts to support your stance. Doing so distinguishes judgment from opinion and contributes to your credibility and professional advancement.

Critical Thinking Questions

1. How would you make the three ineffective research questions effective?
2. How do the three effective research questions help in planning the research process?

FOCUSED RESEARCH QUESTIONS

Once you have formulated your main research question, the next step is to break down the main question into more detailed questions, called **focused research questions.** Focused research questions break down the main question by asking *who, what, where, when, why*, and *how*. These questions keep the research directed to the specifics of the topic and purpose of the question. They allow the researcher to develop a well-planned and efficient search strategy.

Review the focused research questions below, which have been developed for the following main research question:

Does exercise level positively or negatively impact food consumption in obese individuals?

Effective focused questions:

- What is the definition of an obese individual?
- What is the definition of exercise? How is exercise measured?
- Do obese individuals who increase their level of exercise increase or decrease their food intake measured in calories?
- What level of exercise shows a change in food intake?

These focused questions allow you to make a plan for researching the main question. They give you a start on identifying specific resources you can use to find the information. By answering the focused questions, you can begin to organize your thoughts, back up your ideas with information, and logically and reasonably answer the main research question.

2

Reflection Questions

Think about a research project you have completed in the past.

1. What is an effective research question?
2. What are good focused questions you could have asked for this project?

Critical Thinking Questions

1. Consider the example of Charley Murphy and his goal of increasing the technical expertise of his employees that was given at the beginning of the chapter. What are three effective research questions he might use to guide his staff members in their research?
2. What are possible focused questions he could develop to guide his research process?

PRIMARY AND SECONDARY INFORMATION SOURCES

Information sources can be categorized as primary or secondary. **Primary information sources** are those that are closest to the actual event, time period, or individual in question. The information in these sources has not been edited, interpreted, condensed, or evaluated, which might result in a change of the original information. Obviously, the more altered or manipulated the original information is, the more risk there is of error. Primary resources also present original thinking and observations, such as the original research used to write journal articles reporting on original scientific studies, experiments, or observations.

Secondary information sources are those that are removed from the primary source. Authors of secondary sources examine, interpret, or reflect on the primary source information to restate or reuse the information. Secondary sources also act as pointers to the primary sources by referencing the original sources. Secondary information sources are much more available and sometimes easier to use, but they should be critically evaluated to ensure that care has been taken to maintain the integrity of the original information and that the author of a secondary source has not misinterpreted or altered the original information to support a specific opinion or viewpoint.

Use of inaccurate or misleading secondary information can compromise your research. For example, in Charley Murphy's research need discussed earlier, original information would include data from each manufacturer's product guidelines that provide facts about the products. A source of secondary information might be an editorial in a popular magazine criticizing one specific brand of computers. The editorial may or may not be based on facts but could impact the information that Charley's sales force provides to customers. This could result in reduced sales of that computer brand. Keep in mind that all information has the potential to influence some behavior. Therefore, you must ensure that you use information that is accurate, credible, and complete. Chapter 4 further addresses ways to determine the credibility of information.

2

Examples of primary sources:

- Memoirs
- Diaries
- Autobiographies
- Interviews with people
- Public records
- Transcripts of speeches
- Letters, e-mails, memos, listservs, blogs, discussion threads, newsgroups, and other correspondences
- Discussions and electronic discussions on the Internet
- Meetings and minutes to meetings
- Newspaper articles reporting at the time of the event
- Surveys
- Government documents

- Artifacts
- Photographs and works of art
- Observations
- Patents
- Works of literature, such as fiction and poems

Examples of secondary sources:

- Books and textbooks
- Review articles from scholarly journals
- Scientific reports (articles in scholarly journals that describe an original research study, experiment, or observation)
- Technical reports
- Conference papers and proceedings
- Theses and dissertations
- Handbooks
- Databases
- Catalogs and other indexing and abstracting tools used to locate information
- Newspaper articles that analyze events
- Dictionaries and encyclopedias
- Magazine articles
- Newspapers
- Videotapes and audiotapes, CD ROMs, and DVDs that have been edited

2

CRITICAL THINKING QUESTIONS

1. Of the two types of information sources, primary and secondary, which do you think is more accessible? Why?
2. What specific primary information sources might be available for your field of study? List as many examples as you can.
3. What specific secondary information sources are available for your field of study? List as many examples as you can.
4. What are potential issues with using any of these secondary information sources for your field of study?

REFLECTION QUESTION

1. What types of primary source information would authors have at their disposal to research your life?

LIBRARY INFORMATION SOURCES

Once you have thought about the information need and clearly defined the need in terms of a research question and appropriate focused questions, it is time to move to Step 2 in the information process: Find the information. Finding information incorporates two different skills:

1. Being aware of the various sources of information available.
2. Knowing how to locate and access the information in the information source.

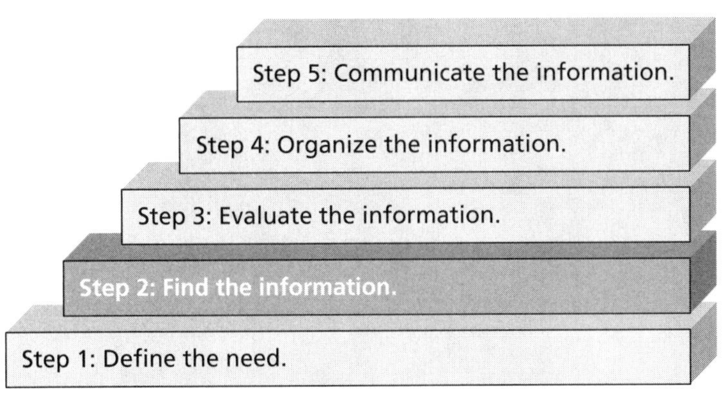

Research Process Step 2: Find the information
The second step of any research project should be to find the information efficiently.

2

Identifying the sources of information that are useful in academic and workplace research is a critical step in conducting an effective information search. Knowledge of information sources available in libraries and on the Internet is the foundation of library literacy, which is an important component of information literacy.

BOOKS

Books are common and convenient sources of information. Books can be **fiction** (content based on imagination and not necessarily on fact) or **nonfiction** (information presented as fact). Books are available on every subject of interest and found in library stacks in most libraries.

Because of the significant time lapse between the time a book is written and its publication, certain types of information found in books may be outdated. For example, information from a book on human anatomy will be valid for years to come, as anatomy does not change quickly. Conversely, a book on computer software is likely to be outdated quickly because of the nature of the information and the rapidly changing technical world. When you select a book as a reference, you will have to use good judgment about the kind of information you are seeking. In the example of computer software, a better and more current choice would be the technical documentation from the most recent version of the software you are researching.

Books are common and convenient sources of information.

2

Fiction

The primary purpose of a work of fiction is entertainment. Fiction gives the reader the opportunity to see problems and solutions through the actions of the character(s). The reader can live vicariously through the novel's characters and gain insight into "real-life" situations without repercussion. Figure 2-1 outlines the elements of fiction.

Historical fiction is based on an event or a sequence of events in history that actually occurred, with people who actually lived or are created within the author's imagination. The author re-creates action

Elements of a Fiction Novel	
Character(s)	Solution to the problem
Plot	Tone/mood
Theme	Symbolism
Setting	Imagery
Point of view	Figurative language
Basic problem	

Figure 2-1 Elements of a Fiction Novel

Numerous elements in a fiction work differentiate it from nonfiction.

Elements of Nonfiction	
Facts	Direct quotes
Characters (Real)	Illustrations
First person accounts	Timelines
Actual events	Maps
Actual places	Table of contents
Photographs	Bibliography
Archival material	Glossary
Charts	Index
Diagrams	

Figure 2-2 Elements of Nonfiction
The elements commonly seen in nonfiction are more factual than creative.

and emotion through imagination to tell the story of the event or of the characters.

Nonfiction

Nonfiction presents factual information. Nonfiction books are based on research and actual events that have occurred, and characters or objects that actually exist now or have existed in the past. Critical evaluation of the information given in a nonfiction resource is vital to the credibility of a research project. Elements that should be considered in light of the goal of your research include the author's background, purpose for writing the book, author's attitude, and the audience for which the work is written. See Figure 2-2 for examples of elements of nonfiction. Evaluation of nonfiction information will be discussed in depth in chapter 4.

REFERENCE SOURCES

A library typically has a **reference section** or **reference desk** (or information desk) that is staffed by a **reference librarian.** Library patrons use the reference services to get answers to questions or to receive assistance with their research needs. The professionally trained librarians who staff the reference desk will help you find the kind of information sources that best meet your needs by conducting a reference interview. In many libraries, you also can call, e-mail, or use online chat to get help.

Use the reference desk to:

- Get help finding a library resource.
- Get the answer to a specific, factual question.
- Get assistance in using the Online Public Access Catalog (OPAC) or other library computer resources.
- Access ready reference books that are commonly used.
- Access rare or restricted items in the library.
- Locate difficult-to-find information.
- Put a library resource on hold when an item you need is temporarily unavailable (i.e., checked out by another patron). The librarian will notify you when the resource has been returned.
- Access resources that instructors have set aside for a specific project or for a specific time period.
- Discover items in the library that are not cataloged in the OPAC, such as old telephone books, college-course catalogs, and school yearbooks.
- Sign up for use of library equipment, such as microform readers or computers.
- Make a recommendation to the library that it purchase something for its collection.
- Ask to be shown exactly where in the library a resource is located. (Most librarians will take you there.)
- Gain access to locked or reserved study or conference rooms.
- Get recommendations on specific resources to meet a specific research need.
- Get recommendations for useful websites or advice on searching the Internet.
- Get a referral to a different library that has additional resources to meet your needs.
- Request a resource from another library through the interlibrary loan system.

A **reference source** is material from which information can be drawn. Reference sources are authoritative and frequently subject-

A reference librarian is an excellent source of information.

specific. Reference resources include reference books, records from library catalogs, general or subject-specific indexes, and bibliographic databases. Many reference materials are available in both print and electronic formats and often are accessible through a local library computer system or via the Internet. Reference sources may provide actual information, or they may be used to find additional information sources. Some of the more commonly available and useful reference sources are outlined below. Typically, reference books cannot be checked out of the library but must be used in the library. In most cases, you can make copies of the information you need, provided that you observe copyright restrictions.

Encyclopedias

An **encyclopedia** is a collection of detailed articles on a wide range of subjects. Encyclopedias typically are used to find background information on a subject. They can be general (e.g., *World Book Encyclopedia*), covering a broad range of topics, or subject-specific (e.g., *Encyclopedia of Psychology*). Subject-specific articles contain detailed articles related to specific fields of study and are written by experts in that field.

Encyclopedias are basic tools that can be good starting points for the research. Topics are arranged in alphabetical order and presented in short- to medium-length essays. The articles sometimes include illustrations or other visual materials and may reference additional articles or suggest related topics of interest. Encyclopedias also may supply keywords to help you narrow or broaden your search. Online encyclopedias can be accessed without charge or for a subscription fee.

An encyclopedia is a collection of detailed articles on a wide range of topics.

Examples of general encyclopedias:

- *World Book Encyclopedia*
- *Academic American Encyclopedia*
- *The Encyclopedia Britannica*
- *The Encyclopedia Americana*
- *The Random House Encyclopedia*
- *The Lincoln Library of Essential Information*
- *The Philips Encyclopedia* (electronic)
- *The New Book of Knowledge*

Examples of subject-specific encyclopedias:

- *World Book Encyclopedia of Peoples and Places*
- *The American Civil War: A Multicultural Encyclopedia*

- *Famous First Facts, International Edition: A Record of First Happening, Discoveries and Inventions in World History*
- *The Encyclopedia of Adoption*
- *U.X.L. Encyclopedia of Biomes*
- *The International Encyclopedia of Adult Education*
- *Advertising Age Encyclopedia of Advertising*
- *The Encyclopedia of Flight*
- *The Encyclopedia of Human Emotions*

Dictionaries

A **dictionary** is an alphabetical listing of words and is used for a quick search of a word or topic to find the word's meaning, spelling, and pronunciation. Dictionaries also include information on parts of speech or word form and word origin. Some dictionaries are general in nature and are useful for basic writing tasks. Others, such as medical dictionaries, are specific to a field of study or topic area. These provide more detailed information similar to that found in an encyclopedia and often include illustrations and other reference-type information.

Additional examples of the hundreds of subject-specific dictionaries are computer-user or technical dictionaries, electronics dictionaries, and slang dictionaries. Numerous electronic dictionaries are available on the Internet without charge.

Examples of general dictionaries:

- *The Oxford English Dictionary*
- *The American Heritage Dictionary*
- *Merriam Webster's Collegiate Dictionary*
- *The World Book Dictionary*
- *The Random House Dictionary of the English Language*
- *Collins English Dictionary* (electronic)

Examples of specific dictionaries:

- *The New Dictionary of Cultural Literacy*
- *The Dictionary of Accounting*
- *The Diabetes Dictionary*

2

- *The Cambridge Aerospace Dictionary*
- *The Historical Dictionary of Afghanistan*
- *The Dictionary of Agriculture*
- *The Rhyming Dictionary*
- *Webster's Biographical Dictionary*
- *Webster's Geographical Dictionary; a Dictionary of Names, of Places with Geographical and Historical Information and Pronunciations.*

Directories

A **directory** is a collection of data organized in a way that allows users to easily access the information. Directories can be alphabetical listings of people, organizations, companies, or institutions. They include addresses, telephone and fax numbers, and other pertinent information. Organizational directories contain member information as well as dates and information for conferences and publications. Common directories are telephone and city directories and the *United States Zip Code Directory*. Many directories are available online with search features that allow the information to be located easily.

Examples of directories commonly used in research:

- *College Blue Book*
- *Biographical Directory of the United States Congress*
- *Bowker's News Media Directory*
- *Martindale-Hubbell Law Directory*
- *Directory of Physicians in the United States*
- *Writer's Market*
- *Sports Market Place Directory*
- *International Sports Directory: The Global Sports Reference Guide*
- *OAG Travel Planner, Hotel & Motel Red Book*
- *U.S. Government Manual*

Almanacs

An **almanac** is a publication that provides statistics, lists, figures, tables, and specific facts in a variety of areas. Almanacs typically are published annually or other regular basis. Almanacs may be general or may be devoted to a specific topic area or field of study. Researchers use almanacs to find and compare current or historical information or statistics. Often, this information is in table form for ease of use. Some online almanacs can be accessed without charge, and others for a subscription fee.

Examples of general almanacs:

- *The World Almanac and Book of Facts*
- *The Encyclopedia Britannica Almanac*
- *Whitaker's Almanac*
- *Information Please Almanac*
- *Encyclopedia Britannica Almanac*
- *Sports Illustrated Almanac*

Examples of subject specific almanacs:

- *The African American Almanac*
- *Days to Celebrate: A Full Year of Poetry, People, History, Holidays, Fascinating Facts and More*
- *Farmer's Almanac*
- *Poor Richard's Almanac*
- *Peterson's College & University Almanac*
- *U.S. Immigration & Migration Almanac*
- *Almanac of American Education*
- *U. X. L. Hispanic American Almanac*
- *Plunkett's Automobile Industry Almanac*
- *Information Please Business Almanac*

Atlases

An **atlas** is a collection of geographical and historical information. Atlases include maps, charts, descriptions, tables, demographic information, natural resources statistics, and data on the physical features of geographical areas. Researchers use atlases to locate places around the world and in outer space, as well as to gather information about the demographics of a region, the physical features of an area or region, or distances between locations. Atlases also are used to plan travel and other recreational activities.

Examples of atlases:

- *World Book Atlas*
- *Atlas of the World* (National Geographic)
- *Atlas of the World* (Oxford University Press)
- *Oxford New Concise World Atlas*
- *Collins World Atlas Gazetteer* (electronic)
- *Atlas of World Affairs*
- *The Kingfisher Student Atlas*
- *Rand McNally Commercial Atlas & Marketing Guide*
- *Color Atlas of Low Back Pain*
- *Scholastic Atlas of Space*
- *Atlas of the Universe*

Indexes

An **index** is an alphabetical list that can be used to find information within a source. An index can be found at the end of a single-volume reference work or nonfiction book. In multivolume reference books, indexes usually are compiled in a separate volume and also may be subject-specific.

Another type of index, the **periodical index,** is a cumulative list of articles from periodicals. Contents are arranged alphabetically by author, title, or subject. An index entry is called a **citation.** Each citation in a periodical index contains information about the article, including the author, article title, and name, volume, issue, and page numbers of the periodical in which the article is published. Periodical indexes may be general in nature, or for a specific topic area, or may combine a group of related disciplines. More will be discussed in chapter 3 about how to use periodical indexes.

Examples of indexes that may be useful in research:

- *Reader's Guide To Periodical Literature*
- *Children's Magazine Guide*
- *Humanities Index*
- *Education Index*
- *Social Science Index*

- *Art Index*
- *Music Index*
- *Alternative Press Index*
- *Business Periodical Index*
- *Book Review Digest*

Other Common Reference Sources

Often called **ready reference sources,** these materials usually are kept at or near the reference desk in a library because of their frequent use. In addition to the reference tools mentioned previously, other common ready reference sources include concordances, handbooks, thesauruses, manuals, and style manuals.

Concordance: an alphabetical list of the most pertinent words in a given text and a notation of where they might be found within that text. Concordances are used for in-depth study of a work or collection. Examples of concordances:

- *A Concordance to Beowulf*
- *A Concordance of the Collected Poems of James Joyce*
- *Exhaustive Concordance of the Bible*

Handbook: a resource that provides concise data, usually in table or chart form on a specialized subject area. A handbook is a useful reference for finding current statistics, procedures, instructions, or specific information on a topic.

Examples of handbooks:

- *A Handbook of Games*
- *Boy Scout Handbook*
- *Brownie Girl Scout Handbook*
- *Young Person's Career Skills Handbook*
- *Handbook of Photography*

Thesaurus: a collection of synonyms, near-synonyms, antonyms (opposite words), phrases, and slang terms for words. A thesaurus can be arranged alphabetically or by idea or concept. As with other resources, specialized thesauruses include specialized expressions for a specific field, such as medicine or computer science. A thesaurus will help you find words to express an idea for which you need to find a different or an opposite word. A typical thesaurus has synonyms for more than 100,000 words. Many thesauruses have unique and helpful features, and you will receive the greatest benefit from the thesaurus you are using by being familiar with its features. Also, many words are not directly interchangeable. A thesaurus and dictionary used together will ensure that you are using the correct word.

At first glance, a thesaurus can look complicated. Therefore, you should start by getting to know your specific thesaurus. Complete instructions typically are found in the introduction. The two main kinds of thesaurus are: (1) a Roget-type that uses a categorization system, and (2) an A–Z type that lists headwords alphabetically. In a Roget-type thesaurus, you look up the word in the index. The index lists the meaning under each word, and a page number next to the meaning you select for the word. Then you go to that page to find synonyms, antonyms, and other information pertaining to the word.

HINT: Look at the word before and the word after each category to ensure that you have reviewed all the possible similar entries. Also, look at all parts of speech. You might see another word with a different part of speech that will help broaden your word search.

In the A–Z listing type of thesaurus, each headword (typically bolded) is listed with its parts of speech (verb, noun, adjective, adverb, etc.) and a concise definition. You will have to consult a dictionary for a more extensive definition. Synonyms are listed under the headword Most words have several meanings. The words listed together under a headword share at least one meaning with the headword. Usually, the first words listed reflect the most common meanings of the word.

HINT: Different words have different connotations, or implied meanings. Be sure you understand the word and its connotation before using it, or you might be saying something you did not intend to say.

Examples of thesauruses:

- *Random House Roget's College Thesaurus*
- *The Thinkers Thesaurus: Sophisticated Alternatives to Common Words*
- *Roget's Descriptive Word Finder*
- *American Heritage Thesaurus for Learners of English*

Manual: similar to a handbook; provides detailed and sometimes "how to" information on specific topics.

Examples of manuals:

- *United States Government Manual*
- *Official Manual of the State of Missouri*

2

Style manual: a writing guide that provides guidelines for writing mechanics and documentation format for research papers and theses. Style manuals are updated continually to keep current with new forms of information. Different styles of citing information sources will be discussed in chapter 6.

Examples of style manuals:

- *The Chicago Manual of Style*
- *New York Times Manual of Style and Usage*
- *MLA (Modern Language Association) Style Manual and Guide to Scholarly Publishing*
- *Publication Manual of the American Psychological Association*
- *Elements of Style*

PERIODICALS

A **periodical** is published on a regular or recurring basis—daily, weekly, monthly, bimonthly, quarterly, or annually. Among periodicals are scholarly journals, popular magazines, trade publications, and newspapers. Periodicals can be issued in print, microform, and electronic formats.

An important feature of a periodical is its currency. Because periodicals are published frequently, they are expected to provide up-to-date information on a topic. The different types of periodicals and the uses of each are summarized next. Evaluation of periodicals is discussed in chapter 4.

Scholarly Journals

A **scholarly journal** typically is published by an educational institution or a professional association. The main goal of a scholarly journal is to disseminate information in a timely manner to professionals and researchers in the field. Scholarly journals often are **peer-reviewed**—sometimes termed **refereed**—which means that the content of the journal has been read with scrutiny and accepted by knowledgeable reviewers who are not on the journal's editorial staff but who work in the field or area discussed in the article. Scholarly journals present reports of original research, experiments, or studies, as well as commentaries, discussions on current issues or events, examinations or analyses of specific topic areas, and reviews of scholarly books or other media in the field of study.

A few examples of the many hundreds of scholarly journals:

- *Journal of the American Medical Association*
- *Harvard Law Review*
- *Journal of Occupational and Environmental Hygiene*
- *The Journal of American Culture*
- *The Journal of Individual Society*
- *Community College Journal*
- *Journal of Sport Management*
- *Journal of Environmental Engineering*
- *School Library Journal*

Popular Magazines

A **popular magazine** provides information on topics of interest to the general public including (but certainly not limited to) news, entertainment, lifestyles, popular culture, leisure reading, parenting, home, science and nature, self-improvement, and do-it-yourself projects. Although some of these magazines provide well-researched and documented information, many do not. The articles typically are short, with no references or substantive information, often providing information of a sensational nature and containing advertisements. The main goal of articles in popular magazine is to sell copies of the magazine itself.

A few examples of the many hundreds of popular magazines:

- *Good Housekeeping*
- *Redbook*
- *Vanity Fair*
- *People*
- *Time*
- *Newsweek*
- *U.S. News & World Report*
- *Vogue*
- *Sports Illustrated*
- *Popular Mechanics*

Trade Publications

A **trade publication** is a periodical for a specific industry or business, usually published by an association tied to the trade. The authors of articles in trade publications typically are practitioners or professionals in a specific field. The goal of these articles is to inform others in the industry.

A few examples of the many hundreds of trade publications:

- *Women's Wear Daily*
- *Valu-line*
- *Furniture World*
- *Hoard's Dairyman*
- *Aramco World*
- *Advertising Age*
- *Stores & Retail Spaces*
- *Chain Store Age*
- *Bobbin*
- *Booklist*

Newspapers

Newspapers are of a local, regional, national, or international venue and are general or topic-specific. They usually cover current news and events. Newspapers may be published by commercial enterprises, by individuals, or by professional organizations to provide information to its members and the public.

A few examples of the many hundreds of newspapers:

- *New York Times*
- *Boston Globe*
- *USA Today*
- *Kansas City Star*
- *St. Louis Post Dispatch*
- *Wall Street Journal*
- *Al Jazeera*

More will be discussed in chapter 4 on how to critically evaluate periodicals.

MULTIMEDIA

Information can be in a form other than print or electronic. Many libraries house or have access to a variety of graphic, audio, video, and film media sources of information. Among these are maps, videotapes, CD ROMs, DVDs, 16-mm films, audiotapes, vinyl records, and so forth. Each library or library system has access to various media or can borrow a desired media resource from another library using the interlibrary loan system.

INFORMATION RETRIEVAL SYSTEMS

Information retrieval systems allow access to electronic resources and information. Electronic resources include online catalogs, databases, indexes, abstracts, and full-text articles in electronic journals, reference sources, and e-books that are stored in an electronic format and accessed by computer. Many forms of information are available electronically.

ONLINE PUBLIC ACCESS CATALOG (OPAC)

A library catalog is a register of all bibliographic items in a specific library or library system. A bibliographic item is any piece of information or information resource that is a library material. In the past, researchers located library holdings by searching a card catalog—a file cabinet containing individual cards with bibliographic information about specific items in the library. Since the mid-1980s, the physical card catalog most often has been replaced with a computerized catalog called an OPAC.

An **online public access catalog (OPAC)** is a computerized online catalog of all the materials held in a library and can be searched quickly and efficiently using a computer. An OPAC provides electronic records of materials that a library owns. OPACs can be searched using author, title, subject, call number, or keyword. Although some libraries still have their original physical card catalogs, few maintain them or use them often.

The purpose of cataloging library resources is to help the library patron find the resource, to show what the library has available, and to provide enough information for the user to make a decision about selecting the resource. Many libraries have made their OPACs accessible via the Internet. Most OPACs are Windows-based and, to simplify the search, use pulldown menus, popup windows, dialog boxes, mouse operations, and graphical user interface components.

Library cataloging follows established cataloging rules that have been designed to ensure consistent cataloging of library materials. Most cataloging rules are based on the International Standard Bibliographic Description (ISBD) produced by the International Federation of Library Associations (IFLA).

DATABASES

A **database** is a collection of digitized information organized for simplified, fast searching and retrieval. Databases are updated regularly and contain bibliographic citations or references for periodicals, books, reports, and other publications. Full-text databases contain these citations as well as the full text of the periodical, book, or report. A database may be general or subject-specific. Vendors of databases are called **aggregators.** An aggregated service simultaneously accesses information from several databases. Examples of those who provide this service are Ebscohost, ProQuest, and the Gale Group. Libraries subscribe to these resources to make information readily available to their staffs and library users. Librarians have access to literally hundreds of databases for all kinds of information. Electronic formats allow convenient searching of the resource using techniques that narrow the search to pinpoint the exact data needed.

Examples of databases:

- *Academic Research Premier:* A database that includes both scholarly and peer-reviewed journals dating back to 1975.
- *Business Source Premiere:* A database that indexes journals related to the many areas of business.

THE INTERNET

2

The **Internet** is a high-speed electronic network that connects personal computers and organizational computer facilities around the world. This network is connected by fiberoptics such as telephone lines, cables, and communications satellites. The Internet is available to anyone with a computer, connections, and an Internet service provider such as AOL, SBC, or Sprint. Many cable companies also provide Internet service. The Internet has been called the "information superhighway" because this network connects millions of computers around the world, allowing users to communicate through e-mail and file transfers. A rich source of information, the Internet allows users to access a limitless amount of data if they have the skills to find this information.

The Internet is a massive information-retrieval system. The **World Wide Web** is an international network of Internet servers that allows access to documents written in HTML (hypertext markup language) and provides links to other documents, graphic files, audio files, video files, and many other forms of information. This means that you can move from one resource to another by clicking on links within a resource. Note that Internet is not synonymous with the World Wide Web. The World Wide Web is something that is available via the Internet, as are e-mail and other Internet services. Consider the World Wide Web to be a read–write information space for Internet resources such as images, text, videos, and other media.

A **website** is made up of a collection of web pages stored in a single folder or within related subfolders of a web server. A **web page** is an electronic resource on the World Wide Web assigned a unique Internet address called a **uniform resource locator** (URL). It is displayed using a web browser such as Internet Explorer. Web pages can contain numerous types of information including text and graphics, audio and video, interactive multimedia, applets (subprograms that run inside the page), links, and downloadable files.

In some cases, the user has to download additional software modules, called **plugins,** and install them on the computer in order to run interactive elements and applets or to display specialized types of data. Hundreds of plugins are available on the Internet, downloadable free of charge. Most specialized software applications for graphics, video, and animation have their own specialized plugins that are required to view their specialized content. In most cases, the web page will have a link and instructions on how to locate and download the needed plugins. Other plugins serve specialized functions on a web page.

Examples of plugins for viewing elements and specialized plugins for web pages:

- *Flash:* allows viewing of rich-media content such as animations and interactive presentations.
- *Quicktime:* enables viewing of video, sound, animation, text, graphics, and so forth.
- *Acrobat Reader:* allows viewing of .pdf files.
- *RealMedia:* enables viewing of video, sound, animation, and graphics including streaming audio and video.
- *ieSpell:* adds a tool to Internet Explorer that spell-checks text input boxes on web pages.
- *AdShield:* blocks banner ads and popups in Internet Explorer.

Web pages also contain content that cannot be seen in a browser. For example, a web page contains scripts (often JavaScript) that add functionality to the page. When you roll the mouse over a place on a page and additional text appears, you are seeing the results of JavaScript. Another unseen element on a web page is a Cascading Style Sheet, which tells how the page is to be formatted. Meta tags provide hidden information about the page itself, providing information to search engines to help in categorizing the page for search purposes.

A **home page** is the main or first screen of a website, with links to other pages on the site. This first page is also called an index page and may be described in that way in the web page's address ending in

2

index.html, or something similar. Many college and university libraries have home pages with links to various research resources, as do many other organizations that provide information to specific industries or to the public in general. On the home page, most libraries include links to online databases and their OPAC.

Many web pages include a **navigation bar** that contains links to other pages on the website, or sometimes to entirely different websites. Navigation bars can be horizontal or vertical, depending upon the design of the website. Typically, the navigation bar is seen on all pages of the website to make it easy to jump from one area to another. If you get to a page that does not have the navigation bar, you can simply click your browser's back button to go back to the page showing the navigation bar. The back button takes you, in order, to the pages visited previously.

Common links on the navigation bar are *About* (provides information about the sponsor of the website), *Home* (takes you to the home page of the site), *Contact Us* (provides contact information), and *Resources* (provides additional resources or external links). Numerous other links might be to company departments, products and services, certificates, publications, and other relevant pages, depending on the purpose and design of the site.

Web Browsers

Although you can view most web pages with any software application that can read text documents, to view a web page as it is intended and to access all of the page's functionality, you must use special software, called a **web browser.** The browser interprets the Internet files and puts them in a readable format. There are many different web browsers with different capabilities. Even different versions of the same web browser have different capabilities.

Examples of commonly used browsers:

- Netscape Navigator
- Internet Explorer
- Mozilla
- Mozilla Firefox
- Opera

Search Engines

Because there are millions of Internet sites, we must have an efficient way to search for the information and sites we need. **Search engines** use computer software that makes the World Wide Web searchable using keywords or phrases. Search results may be listed by relevancy, by currency, or by some other method. The Internet has many different search engines that can be used to find information, but because each search engine allows searching through only those files in its specific database, using only one search engine provides only a small portion of the available sites on the Internet. To find a more complete list of Internet sites, **metasearch engines** search multiple individual search engines simultaneously. For extensive information, ratings, and tips on using search engines effectively, go to SearchEngineWatch on the Internet.

Examples of commonly used search engines:

- Yahoo
- Google
- AltaVista
- AdvanceSearch
- NorthernLight
- Powersearch
- Alltheweb
- Hotbot
- Ask.com
- Monstercrawler
- Dogpile
- Ixquick
- Highway61
- MetaGopher

HINT: Keep in mind that when you are using a search engine, you are not searching the entire Internet; you are searching a portion of it.

2

Critical Thinking Questions

1. How do online search engines work?
2. How might different search engines affect the results of a search? (This might take some research!)
3. Is the large number of results from an Internet search a bad thing? Why?
4. Under what circumstances might you want to limit the number of results you receive?

Internet Information Resources

As stated earlier, many resources available in a physical library are now available on the Internet via virtual libraries, subject directories, and individual websites. Many of the resources are free, and others are fee-based or subscription services. Some of the more useful Internet information sources are explored in more depth here.

Internet Subject Directories

Another important tool on the Internet is a **subject directory,** a collection of links to a large number of Internet resources, typically organized by topic area. Commercial subject directories are general in nature and are much less selective. Academic and professional directories usually are maintained by experts and cater to professionals who need credible information.

Examples of Internet subject directories:

- INFOMINE (http://infomine.ucr.edu)
- The Internet Public Library (www.ipl.org)
- Librarians' Index to the Internet (http://lii.org)

Online Reference Resources

An information-literate individual can easily access online reference resources such as dictionaries, thesauruses, encyclopedias, almanacs, handbooks, directories, and so forth via the Internet. Fee structures for these resources vary from no charge to an annual or monthly subscription charge. Some sites are free but require a registration, and others allow free use of basic services while charging a fee for more advanced or expanded services.

Examples of useful reference resources on the Internet:

- Refdesk (www.refdesk.com)
- Questia (www.questia.com)
- Merriam-Webster Online (www.m-w.com)
- Gove Dictionary of Art (www.goveart.com)
- Encyclopedia.com (www.encyclopedia.com)
- Occupational Outlook Handbook (www.bls.gov/oco/home.htm)

HINT: For reference resources that you find that you use often, consider putting the links to the site on your computer's desktop so you can access them easily.

Online Periodicals

As discussed earlier in the chapter, a single library does not subscribe to every available periodical. An alternative to using your library's periodicals is to find a full-text version of the article online. The general procedure to search for full-text articles is basically the same as that for a physical library. Use an online periodical index to find the needed citation information. In many cases, the actual full-text article can be accessed directly from the citation. Some full-text articles are available free, and others must be purchased. Many online libraries and subject directories also link to periodical indexes and the articles themselves.

Examples of periodical sites on the Internet:

- PubMed Central (www.pubmedcentral.nih.gov)
- HighBeam (www.highbeam.com)
- NewsLink (http://newslink.org)
- FindArticles (www.findarticles.com)

Web Portals

A **web portal,** sometimes called a **gateway,** is a site on the Internet that provides links to many different kinds of information. Some portals are general in nature, and others provide links to information in a specific topic area, such as business, computers, law, or medicine. On a web portal, you can find industry-related information, products, news, periodicals, organizations, chat rooms, people finders, and almost anything else related to the industry and found on the Internet. Some web portals are maintained by Internet Service Providers (e.g., AOL and Yahoo!), and others are maintained by states, professional organizations, or special interest groups. There are hundreds, if not thousands, of web portals for almost every industry.

Examples of web portals on the Internet:

- AOL (www.aol.com)
- About (www.about.com)
- Forbes (www.forbes.com)
- FirstGov (www.firstgov.com)

Professional and Trade Organizations

Professional and trade organizations are groups of professionals with similar interests or positions. These organizations are excellent sources for current information in an industry, for trends and current practices, for licensure and certification information, and for networking with other professionals who have similar interests. Most organizations have some kind of online presence and offer excellent and credible information on their websites. Information-literate individuals can keep current in their field by participating in professional organizations and by reviewing these websites regularly. A good starting place to find appropriate professional organization websites is with Google's directory listing for professional organizations.

Examples of professional organizations:

- Information Technology Association of America (ITAA) (www.itaa.org)
- Computer Technology Industry Association (CompTIA) (www.comptia.org)
- American Health Information Management Association (AHIMA) (www.ahima.org)
- American Association of Medical Assistants (AAMA) (www.aama-ntl.org)
- National Cosmetology Association (NCA) (www.behindthechairexchange.com/nca)

REFLECTION QUESTIONS

1. What professional organizations are appropriate for your field?
2. What information do these organizations maintain on their websites?

In the scenario presented at the beginning of this chapter, Charley Murphy had a goal of helping his staff members improve their product knowledge so they can provide better overall customer services and improve sales. By understanding how to formulate a search statement and then develop focused research questions, Charley can teach his staff members to be efficient in researching their equipment.

Also, by understanding the various places to find information both physically at a library and on the Internet, Charley can help them become more information-literate and increase their professionalism as employees.

learning activities

Activity #1: Resource Exploration

STEP 1: Review your library resources, consult with the reference librarian at your local library or school library, and search the Internet to complete the Resource Table for your field of study.

STEP 2: Continue to add to the list as you find additional resources, and keep this table electronically for reference as you conduct research and locate additional resources.

Resource Table

Resource Type	Resource Name	Resource Location and Access Instructions	Description
Primary Information Sources			
Secondary Information Sources			
Nonfiction Books			
General Encyclopedias			
Subject-Specific Encyclopedias			
General Dictionaries			
Subject-Specific Dictionaries			
Directories			
Almanacs			
Atlases			

(Continued)

2

Resource Table (*Continued*)

Resource Type	Resource Name	Resource Location and Access Instructions	Description
Indexes			
Concordances			
Handbooks			
Thesaurus			
Manuals			
Scholarly Journals			
Popular Magazines			
Trade Publications			
Databases			

Activity #2: Database Exploration

STEP 1: Using your library's resources, explore the databases that are available. Usually these will include a short description of the database. Some libraries list databases in alphabetical order and by subject covered.

STEP 2: Thinking of your field of study, make a list of the specific databases that are appropriate for your research.

Activity #3: Search Engine Comparison

STEP 1: Do a search for a limited topic of your choice using a search engine, and then do the same search using a metasearch engine.

STEP 2: Compare and contrast the results. What is the difference in the number of results of your search? What is the difference in the type of results or sites that are returned?

STEP 3: Note which search engine(s) best meets your needs.

Activity #4: Internet Resource Exploration

STEP 1: Explore the Internet to complete the Internet Resource Table for your field of study.

STEP 2: Continue to add to the list as you find additional resources, and keep this table electronically for reference as you conduct resources.

Internet Resource Table

Resource Type	Resource Name	Resource URL and Access Instructions	Description
Web Browsers			
Common Plugins for Your Browser			
Search Engines			
Internet Subject Directories			
Online Reference Resources			
Online Periodicals			
Web Portals			
Professional and Trade Organizations			

2

LEARNING OBJECTIVES REVISITED

Review the learning objectives for this chapter and rate your level of achievement for each objective, using the rating scale provided. For each objective on which you do not rate yourself as a 3, outline a plan of action that you will take to fully achieve the objective. Include a timeframe for this plan.

1 = did not successfully achieve objective
2 = understand what is needed but need more study or practice
3 = achieved learning objective thoroughly

	1	2	3
Explain the need for a main research question and relevant, focused research questions.	☐	☐	☐
Develop effective main research questions and focused research questions.	☐	☐	☐
Differentiate between primary and secondary information sources.	☐	☐	☐
Explain various ways information is presented.	☐	☐	☐
Explain various ways you can access information.	☐	☐	☐
Identify and describe common information sources.	☐	☐	☐

Steps to Achieve Unmet Objectives

Steps	Due Date
1. ____________________	__________
2. ____________________	__________
3. ____________________	__________
4. ____________________	__________

POTENTIAL ITEMS FOR LEARNING PORTFOLIO

Refer to the "Developing Portfolios" section at the front of this textbook for more information on learning portfolios. Consider adding the following results from this chapter's learning activities or even ideas of your own to your learning protfolio.

- Resource Table
- Database Exploration List
- Comparison of Search Engine Report

CHAPTER OUTLINE

3 How Do You Find and Access Information?

THE BIG PICTURE

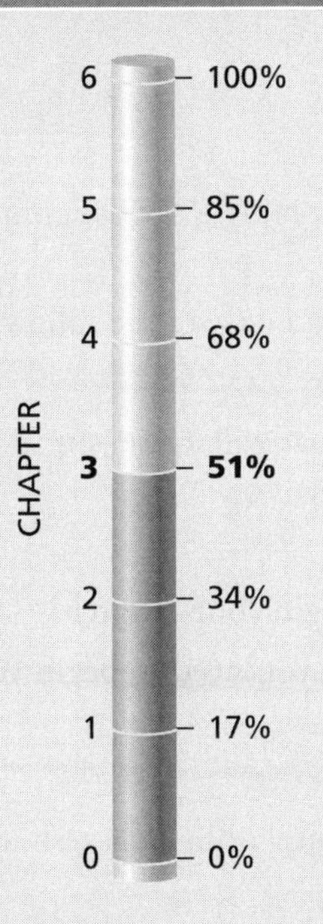

LEARNING OBJECTIVES

By the end of this chapter, students will achieve the following objectives:

- Use several techniques to search for relevant information efficiently.
- Identify several common sources for information.
- Use library resources to find and access information.
- Explain the importance of having a method for collecting information.

CHAPTER 3 SCENARIO

©2007 JupiterImages Corporation

An information-literate professional must know how to access and organize information that is found.

Knowing what types of information are available and where to find them is only the first step in conducting research. The next vital step is to access and organize the information. Consider the following scenario, which emphasizes the process of accessing and collecting information.

Danielle Watson has been given an assignment to write a research paper for her college history course. Her professor has allowed free choice on the selection of topics. Danielle has learned about using the library and its resources, but this is the first time she has been instructed to write a paper that requires her to put this information to use. For this assignment, the professor requires that the students use specific resources, both primary and secondary sources. The required resources include

- five nonfiction books
- five reference resources
- appropriate indexes
- two general databases
- two subject-specific databases
- four scholarly journals
- three credible websites

What plan does Danielle have to make to complete the assignment successfully?

Imagine yourself in Danielle's position and answer the following questions:

- What can you bring from chapter 2 that will assist you in beginning your research?
- What should your first step be?
- Who could you consult with as you begin your research?
- What kinds of information sources do you need to begin your research?
- Where do you find these resources?
- How do you search for the information within each resource?

- What information-gathering strategies can be used?
- How well do you think you would be able to complete this project efficiently (without wasting a lot of time)?

If we value the pursuit of knowledge, we must be free to follow wherever that search may lead us. The free mind is not a barking dog, to be tethered on a ten-foot chain.

— Adlai E. Stevenson Jr. (1900–1965)
speech at the University of Wisconsin, Madison, October 8, 1952

LIBRARY ORGANIZATION

Even with an effective research question and several focused research questions that serve to narrow the research scope sufficiently, finding the right information still can be a daunting task. Review again the steps in the Research Process shown below. To complete Step 2: Find the Information, you first must understand how libraries are organized, how the materials in libraries and on the Internet are cataloged and referenced, and how to access and efficiently use these reference tools. A closer look at the complex library organization system will help you understand its structure and how to use it effectively.

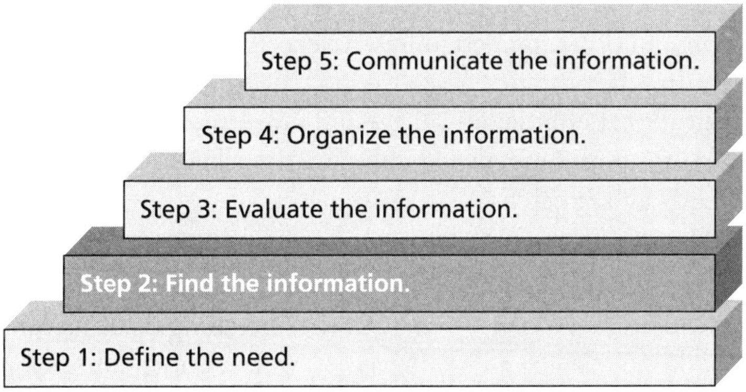

Step 5: Communicate the information.
Step 4: Organize the information.
Step 3: Evaluate the information.
Step 2: Find the information.
Step 1: Define the need.

Research Process Step 2

The second step of any research project should be to efficiently find the information.

As discussed in chapter 2, libraries organize their holdings using a **library catalog,** which is a log or register of all the items in the library. Materials in a library are referred to as **bibliographic items.** A library item can be any piece of information, such as a book, a graphic, a map, an audiotape or videotape, a computer file, and so on. Before the computer came into extensive use in the 1980s, libraries physically documented their library catalog using a **card catalog.** A card catalog is a large set of physical file cabinets holding a **catalog record** (small index card) containing each library item's relevant information. Information on the catalog record includes the call number, the author, title, edition, publisher, brief physical description of the item, notes about the item's content, and a valid Library of Congress subject heading assigned to the item. The file cabinets are organized so you can search using different types of information, such as by author, title, or subject.

Nearly all physical card catalogs have been replaced by a convenient computer system—Online Public Access Catalog (OPAC). Although some libraries still retain their card catalogs, few libraries update these physical catalogs. You might see a sign posted stating the last year the card catalog was updated. More current information then would reside on the OPAC. Some libraries have removed their card catalogs altogether to make space for additional book stacks or technology.

We discussed OPACs in depth in chapter 2, and the following is a review of important points to keep in mind.

OPACs catalog the holdings of a specific library or library system. Each library or library system has access to various resources. Some libraries house information pertaining to a specific area, such as medicine or law. In other libraries the collection is designed for the general public. Educational libraries on college and university campuses contain holdings for both the general public and the school's specific programs of study and research.

OPACs do not catalog information within a specific library holding. In many cases libraries lend materials to patrons of a different library through the interlibrary loan system. OPACs, including those that are web-based, do not catalog all holdings everywhere, only holdings for that specific library or library system. For example, an OPAC will catalog a library's specific journal holding, such as the *Journal of the American Medical Association*. The library will not catalog a specific article published in that journal. To find specific articles, a periodical index is required. Indexes will be discussed shortly.

OPACs do not catalog all of the items in a library. Many libraries store informational items that are not cataloged. These items might include local historical documents, old phone books, school yearbooks, folders of newspaper clippings, manuscripts, photographs, map collections, pamphlets, and so forth. Different libraries have different holdings catalogs. In some cases the library is in process of cataloging holdings. (If you are looking for these kinds of items, ask the reference librarian.)

OPACs allow for searching using several criteria. These criteria include the author of the work, the title of the work, the official designated subject heading, and keywords.

Many other resources are available outside a library or library system on the Internet. In addition to OPACs, which make searching for a library's resources convenient and efficient, you can access many valuable information sources via the Internet. Information-literate individuals understand both library and nonlibrary resources and how to locate and access these resources efficiently.

Throughout the course of your education or career, you likely have used many print resources such as books and periodicals. Libraries have many nonprint materials as well. Nonprint materials are items that are published in any format other than paper and may or may not be cataloged in the OPAC. To use any of these items, ask the reference librarian for help.

Nonprint Resources Commonly Found in a Library	
Computer files	Compact discs
Sound recordings	CD-ROMs
Visual materials	Cassette tapes
Computer disks	Video tapes (videocassettes)
Video Discs	Laserdiscs
Internet files	Vinyl records
Models	Motion pictures (film reels)
Slides	Photographs
Kits	Microform

Nonprint Resources Commonly Found in a Library

LIBRARY ORGANIZATION

Libraries use two major library cataloging systems to classify their materials: the **Library of Congress Classification System** and the **Dewey Decimal System (DDS).** Both systems organize information into subject categories that facilitate access and retrieval. A third category is the **Superintendent of Documents Classification System (SuDoc),** which many state governments use for their publications. Libraries use these classification systems to assign a call number to individual library holdings. A **library holding** is any material or information that is available in the library. The **call number** is the resource's "address" or location in the library. Call numbers use a combination of numbers and letters indicating the material's subject and shelving location.

LIBRARY OF CONGRESS CLASSIFICATION SYSTEM

Because of the scope and size of even a small library's collection, a broad classification tool is needed. Most academic and research libraries use the Library of Congress Classification System to arrange materials on the shelves. This system was developed in the early 1900s by the Library of Congress to organize the vast amounts of materials in that library. The Library of Congress is our national library and makes its resources available to the American people. It contains more than 130 million items (books and other printed materials, recordings, photographs, maps, and manuscripts) on more than 530 miles of bookshelves in three buildings in Washington, DC. (Billington, n.d.) As mentioned, the Library of Congress organizes its information using Library of Congress Subject Headings (LCSH). Many libraries across the country also use these headings to keep their holdings consistent with the national library.

The Library of Congress Classification System is made up of 21 broad categories. Using most of the alphabet, the divisions are assigned a letter, and then subdivided by numbers. See Figure 3-1 for the major 21 categories.

As discussed earlier, the Library of Congress has defined specific terms and phrases to organize library materials consistently in the national library as well as in libraries across the country. The terms and

A – General Works
B – Philosophy, Psychology, Religion
C – Auxiliary Sciences of History
D – History (general) and History of Europe
E – History: America
F – History: America
G – Geography, Anthropology, Recreation
H – Social Sciences
J – Political Science
K – Law
L – Education
M– Music and Books on Music
N – Fine Arts
P – Language and Literature
Q – Science
R – Medicine
S – Agriculture
T – Technology
U – Military Science
V – Naval Science
Z – Bibliography, Library Science, Information Resources (general)

Figure 3-1 Library of Congress Subject Headings

phrases are called **subject headings,** and these are divided further into more precise headings called **subheadings.** Subheadings are noted by additional letter(s) and are further divided into highly specific sections noted by numbers. If a library item deals with more than one major topic, it may have multiple subject headings. The Library of Congress Classification System is used both to describe the item by subject and to physically organize the item in the library in some libraries.

DEWEY DECIMAL CLASSIFICATION SYSTEM

An alternative library classification system is the **Dewey Decimal System (DDS),** designed by Melville Dewey in 1876. Dewey was a librarian who wanted to create a uniform and efficient way to organize information that the public could easily use. As with the Library of Congress Classification System, like topics are grouped into numbered categories ranging from 000 to 900. These ten categories are

000 — Generalities
100 — Philosophy and Psychology
200 — Religion
300 — Social Science
400 — Language
500 — Natural Science and Mathematics
- 510 — Mathematics
- 520 — Astronomy and allied sciences
- 530 — Physics
- 540 — Chemistry and allied sciences
- 550 — Earth sciences
- 560 — Paleontology and paleozoology
- 570 — Life sciences
- 580 — Botanical sciences
- 590 — Zoological sciences

600 — Technology (applied sciences)
700 — The Arts
800 — Literature and Rhetoric
900 — Geography and History

Figure 3-2 Dewey Decimal System

Ten categories represented in the Dewey Decimal System, each category with numerous subcategories to break down the topics further.

further divided into progressively more precise subdivisions using whole and decimal numbers starting with the main class number. Figure 3-2 shows the ten broad categories or classes in the Dewey Decimal System. Many libraries use the Dewey Decimal System instead of the Library of Congress Classification System to identify, catalog, and physically organize their resources (Online Computer Library Center, 2006).

Records for each individual item contain several useful pieces of information about the resource, which allows the user to assess the usefulness of the library item before actually locating it and seeing it. Records can include

- call numbers
- author(s)
- title or subtitles

- publication information
- brief abstract or summary
- number of pages
- related subjects
- series title

SUPERINTENDENT OF DOCUMENTS CLASSIFICATION SYSTEM

Another type of classification system that is used by the U.S. Government Printing Office to classify publications is the **Superintendent of Documents Classification System,** or **SuDoc.** Many state governments use a modified form of this classification system for their publications. This system uses letters, numbers, and other characters for its call numbers.

3

USING LIBRARY CLASSIFICATION SYSTEMS

To efficiently search for and locate information in a library, the user has to understand the basic principles of and information provided by these classification systems.

CALL NUMBER

Most libraries label each library item with a call number that provides sufficient information to organize the item logically, then physically locate the item. A call number is like a library item's address that tells exactly where the item is located in a given library. The call number typically is found on a label on the spine or outside front cover (for small items) of the item itself. By understanding the call number and the specific classification system used at that library, you should be able to go to the exact location of the item in the library facility. Examples of a call number for each classification system are given in Figure 3-3 and Figure 3-4.

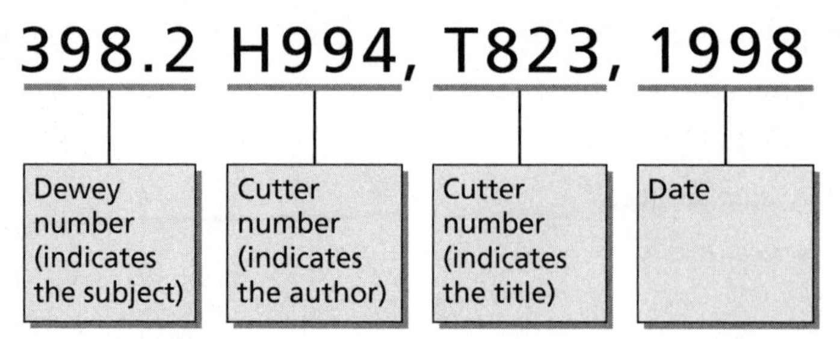

Figure 3-3 Dewey Decimal System Call Number

A call number in the Dewey Decimal System reflects the subject, the author, the title, and the date of publication.

3

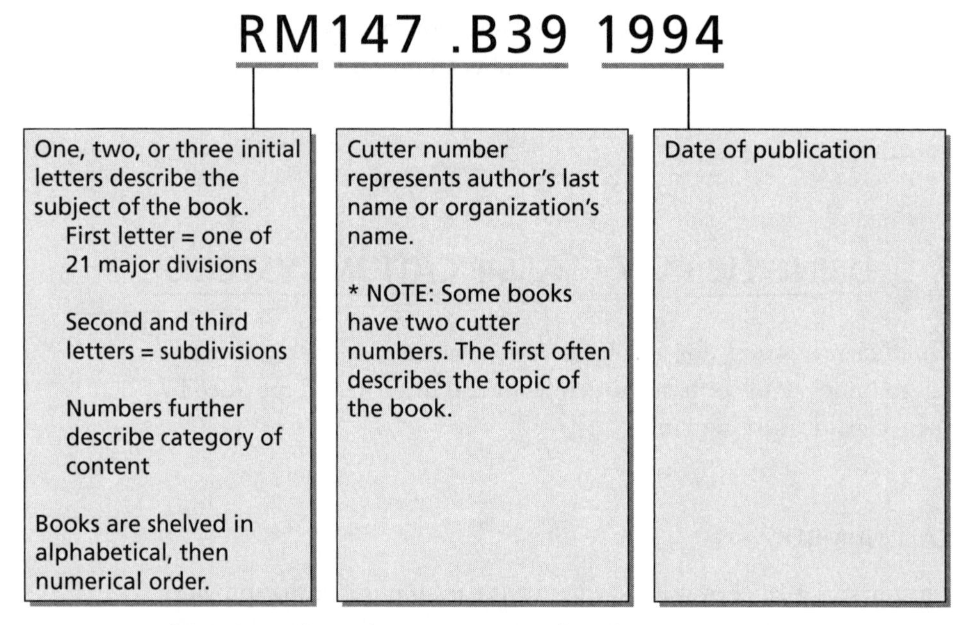

Figure 3-4 Library of Congress System Call Number

A call number in the Library of Congress System reflects the subject, the author, and the date of publication.

LIBRARY STACKS

Libraries organize, shelve or store, and catalog materials on the same subjects together in a specific order using their established cataloging system. The cataloging system describes the items available at a specific library (or library system) in detail and tells where these items are

Libraries organize their holdings in stacks or store materials in secured areas.

located physically in a specific library facility. Materials are organized by subject matter, meaning that materials on the same topic can be found together in one place in the library. To find out where an item is located, you must have the call number for the item. With this call number, you can easily locate the item physically in the library stacks or other storage areas.

Figure 3-5 and Figure 3-6 show how items might be shelved in each classification system.

REFLECTION QUESTIONS

1. Which type of classification system does your library use?
2. Consider how you may have used your library's OPAC in the past. How would you use this resource differently when you are using it for research purposes? Why?

Figure 3-5 Dewey Decimal System Shelf Order: Example

Resources are shelved in the library stacks according to the Dewey Decimal System call number if the library uses this classification system.

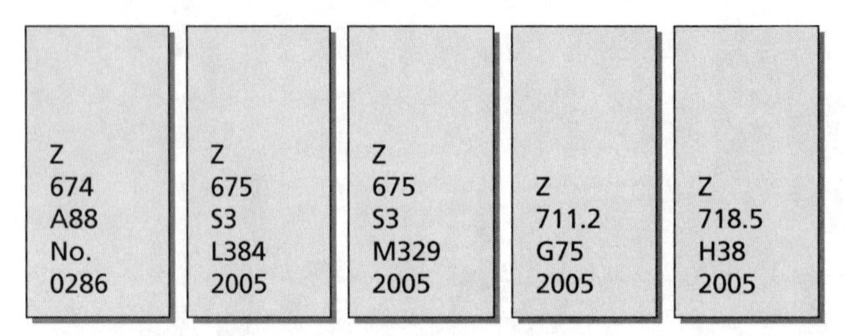

Figure 3-6 Library of Congress Shelf Order: Example

Resources are shelved in the library stacks according to the Library of Congress call number if the library uses this classification system.

SEARCHING FOR INFORMATION

As discussed in chapter 2, search tools such as OPACs, databases, indexes, and so forth help researchers find information. Understanding basic search techniques is essential to be able to use these tools effectively. The first step in conducting an effective search for information is to know the types of information available for most library resources. Most library resources include four pieces of information.

1. Author
2. Title
3. Subject
4. Keyword

Specific strategies for searching using each of these information types are described below.

AUTHOR SEARCH

An **author search** is used to locate works by the author. You need to know at least the author's last name. Any additional information, such as the first and middle name or initials, will help to limit the number of items you find within your search. For example, to find writings by James Michener, you could search using any of the following names:

Michener

Michener, J

Michener, James

By providing as much information as you can, you make your search more efficient because you limit the number of results you have to sort through. In many cases, a work is authored by more than one person. If there is more than one author, use all of the names to limit the search appropriately.

Authors can be people, groups of people, or organizations. When searching for materials published by an organization, you can search by the organization's name, part of the name, and often the acronym for the organization. For example, if you want to search for materials written or published by the American College of Sports Medicine, you would use any of the following terms to start your search:

American

American College

American College of Sports

American College of Sports Medicine

ACSM

Obviously, the more accurately you describe the organization by using all of the words in the name, the more limited your search results will be, making the search more efficient.

TITLE SEARCH

A **title search** is used to locate specific titles of books, references, periodicals, and other resources. If you know the title or part of the title of the book or material for which you are searching, a title search is appropriate. For example, if you are searching for the book *The DaVinci Code,* you could use the following search terms to locate the book quickly:

The DaVinci Code

DaVinci Code

DaVinci

Keep in mind that the more accurate and complete the information you use for your search terms, the fewer will be the number of items appearing in your search results. Probably, many books and other materials have DaVinci in the title. By supplying the full title—The DaVinci Code—you will limit your search results significantly and save time that otherwise would be required to sort through all of the results to find exactly what you want.

HINT: Most catalogs ignore the initial articles "A," "An," and "The."

SUBJECT SEARCH

A **subject search** is used to find materials on a specific topic. Standardized subject headings are assigned by the Library of Congress, and these subject headings are listed in the *Library of Congress Subject Headings (LCSH)* publication. This multivolume set typically is found at the reference desk of the library. It provides synonyms for the subject, as well as related terms to narrow or broaden your search. The *LCSH* also provides references that will direct you to the specific subject heading that is used for a general topic. For example, if you are searching for "farming," the LC subject information would say "see Agriculture," directing you to search under the general topic of "Agriculture." If you were to search for "musicians," you would be directed to use a more specific category related to that term. The *LCSH* listing might provide the information "see Jazz Musicians" or "see American Musicians."

In addition, the LCSH organizes large subjects logically into categories to direct you to the correct subject listing. Sample subject headings for "animal" include

Animal equality
Animal ethics
Animal experimentation
Animal rights
Animal rights activists

An author can be a subject as well as the author of a work. The more information you provide, the more accurate the search results will be. To find items *about* an author, you would treat the author as a subject and search by the author's last name, as in

Shakespeare, William
Dickinson, Emily
Thoreau, Henry David

3

CRITICAL THINKING QUESTION

1. What do you think the results would be if you were to use just the term "Brown" as the subject search term without "Larry" in your search for information about Larry Brown, a contemporary author?

An examination of the *Library of Congress Subject Headings* information will provide insight into how the headings are used. Review Figure 3-7. The subject for this entry is "Mental Illness." The listing provides a brief description of the kinds of information that might be found under the "Mental illness" subject, then gives several abbreviations to help you find additional subject headings that might be more appropriate for your search.

Mental illness (*May Subd Geog*)

Here are entered popular works and works on social aspects of mental disorders. Works on the legal aspects of mental illness are under Insanity. Works on clinical aspects of mental disorders, including therapy, are entered under Psychiatry.

UF Diseases, Mental
Madness
Mental disorders
Mental diseases
BT Diseases
Psychiatry
Psychology, Pathological
RT Mental health
NT Dual diagnosis
Genius and mental illness
Insanity
Neurobehavioral disorders
— **Alternative treatment**
— **Diagnosis**
BT Psychodiagnostics
NT Psychiatric disability evaluation
— Epidemiology
USE Psychiatric epidemiology
— **Prevention**
— Surgery
USE Psychosurgery
— **Treatment** (May Subd Geog)
— **Evaluation**
NT Psychiatric rating scales

Figure 3-7 LCSH Subject Entry

An LCSH subject entry helps a researcher to narrow down a larger topic to specifically locate a library resource by how it is classified.

LCSH abbreviations include:

- *May Subd Geog:* This notation indicates that the subject may be geographically subdivided, meaning that other subject listings may be more closely related to your specific search subject. The hyphens indicate a subdivision.
- *UF:* This abbreviation denotes *unauthorized headings.* The common subjects listed here are not used in the LCSH subject list, and you will waste your time using these search terms to look for your resources. In the example of "Mental illness" in Figure 3-7, the common terms of "Diseases, Mental," "Madness," "Mental disorders," and "Mental diseases" would not be effective search terms.
- *BT:* This abbreviation stands for *broader topic,* a more general topic. This notation gives subject listings that are broader than "Mental illness." If "Mental illness" has too few resources, you can try the subject headings in the BT list. In this example, you might look under the subjects of "Diseases," "Psychiatry," or "Psychology, Pathological."
- *RT:* This abbreviation means *related topic*. The subjects under the RT abbreviation are associated with the main subject, but fall outside of the main term's hierarchy. If you are not finding what you want using "Mental illness," you might try "Mental health" in this example.
- *NT:* This abbreviation means *narrower topic*. The subjects listed under the NT notation are search terms that can be used that are more specific. If you find too many resources under the main subject of "Mental illness," you might narrow your search by using one of the subjects under the NT notation.
- *SA:* This abbreviation (not seen in the Figure 3-7 example) stands for *see also.* Subjects under the SA notation cover similar subjects.
- *USE:* This notation gives information about the correct subject heading in the LCSH listing. For example, if you see, under the subject "Mental Illness," that you might want to look up "surgery," the *USE* notation tells you that Psychosurgery is the appropriate heading for subjects about surgery and mental illness. Understanding this notation could save a significant amount of time by pointing you in precisely the right direction.

- *Hyphens:* All of the subject headings noted with a hyphen are subdivisions of the major listing to help you focus on the exact area of mental illness you want to explore.

KEYWORD SEARCH

If you do not know an author or title, you can conduct a **keyword search.** The difference between a keyword and a subject is that the subject is limited to the specific Library of Congress subject heading assigned to the item, whereas a keyword is any word or word combination in the record.

A keyword search looks for specific keywords in all fields in a record and is used when you have a word or a combination of words that you would like to look for simultaneously. In an OPAC, the keyword could be in the title, the author's name, the subject, or other places in the record. On the Internet, a keyword search brings up results that have that word or word combination anywhere in the document.

BOOLEAN OPERATORS

Boolean operators include the words "and," "or," and "not." These terms can be used in combination with keywords to broaden or narrow the search results by specifying exactly how you want the search to be conducted. Boolean operators can be used with most search engines, databases, and OPACs. A clear understanding of how these simple operators work can save a lot of time in using electronic searching tools.

Boolean operators work like a **Venn diagram** with words. A Venn diagram uses circles that stand alone or overlap to show logical relationships between concepts or ideas. Suppose you want to conduct a search using the search terms "film" and "theater." Each Boolean operator will narrow or broaden your search using keywords.

Figure 3-8 shows the use of the Boolean operator "AND." The operator "AND" is used to search for information on both film *and* theater. The results using these two keywords and the operator "AND" will bring up information that includes both film and theater. The correct notation you would use as your search terms would be *film AND theater*. The results would fall into the middle shaded area created by the overlapping of the film and theater circles. There would

Reflection Question

1. What are some synonyms for the topic "Mental illness" that you could use as an alternative search term? Go to the library and try it yourself using the *Library of Congress Subject Headings* publication.

Reflection Question

1. What key terms or term combinations could you use for a topic that you might be asked to research in your job or a course? Write down at least ten key terms or term combinations that you could use to conduct a keyword search.

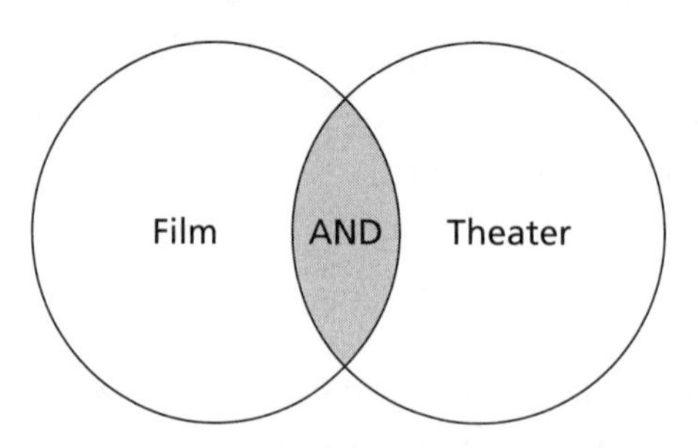

Figure 3-8 Boolean Searching Using "AND"

Using the Boolean operator "and" gives the results that include both search terms.

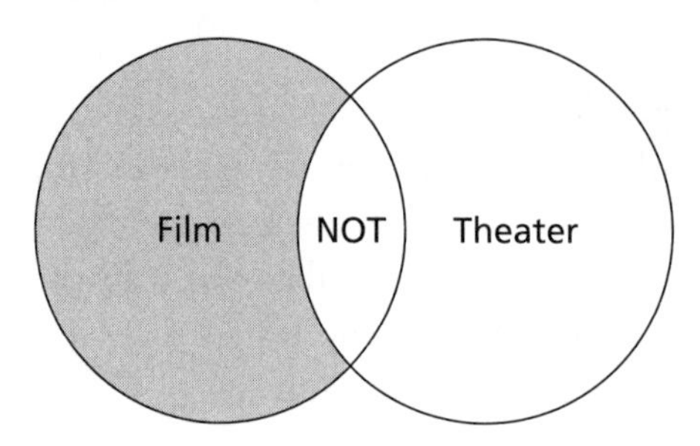

Figure 3-9 Boolean Searching Using "NOT"

Using the Boolean operator "not" gives the results that include one search term but not the other.

be no results for only film and no results for only theater. This operator obviously narrows the search by finding results that include both film and theater.

Figure 3-9 shows use of the Boolean operator "NOT." The "NOT" operator is used when you want to bring up information with one of the keywords but you do not want information that includes the other keyword. In this example, searching for *film NOT theater* results in information about film only and does not bring up information about theater. Any results about film but also including the term "theater" will be omitted. This obviously narrows the search significantly, saving time that might be wasted in sorting through information on film that also includes theater.

Figure 3-10 shows the Boolean operator "OR," which can be used to broaden a search. For example, "theater" has the accepted alternate spelling of "theatre." If you want to make sure that the search returns information using both spellings, you would use the Boolean operator "OR," as in *theater OR theatre*. This will return information that includes both spellings of the word.

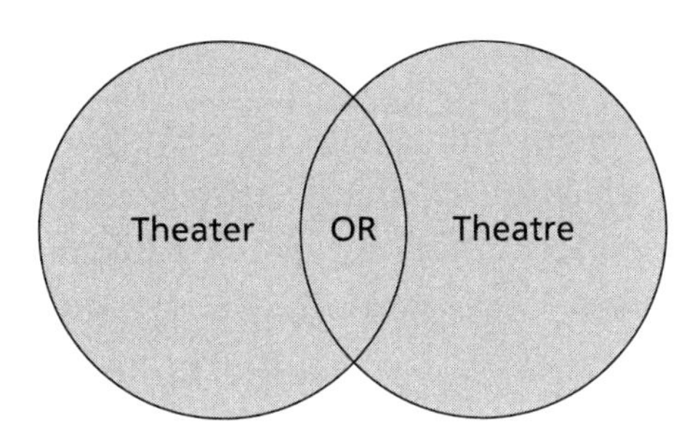

Figure 3-10 Boolean Searching Using "OR"

Using the Boolean operator "or" gives results that include one search term or the other search term, or both.

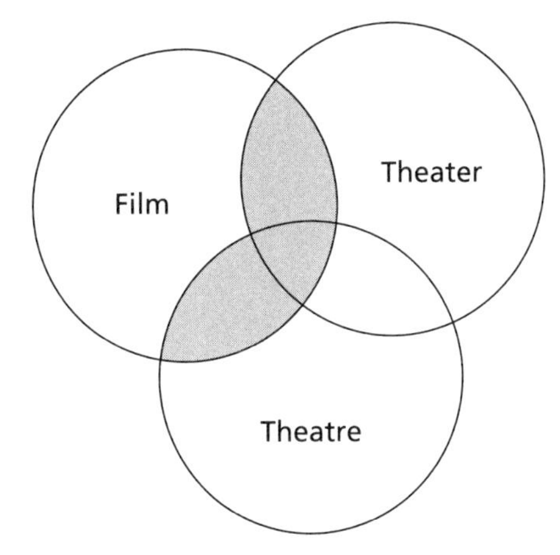

Figure 3-11 Boolean Searching Using "AND" and "OR"

Using the Boolean operator "or" in combination with "and" expands your search.

Combining Boolean operators can be useful at times. For example, if you want to search for information about film and either spelling of theater, you could use the "AND" operator combined with the "OR" operator, as in *film AND (theater OR theatre)*, as illustrated in Figure 3-11.

Implied Boolean operators include + in front of a word to retrieve results when the word is included and a − in front of the word to retrieve results where the word is excluded—similar to AND and NOT operators. Quotation marks around phrases sometimes are used to retrieve results when the specific phrase is included. On the Internet, most search engines have an "Advanced Search" link that provides a way to focus or narrow the searches. These advanced search tips and tools explain the specific search language used by that specific search tool.

Reflection Questions

Go back to your own workplace research example.

1. Using the keywords you listed and other appropriate terms, how could you narrow or broaden your search using only one operator?
2. How can you combine your search terms using the Boolean technique to broaden your search? To narrow your search?

INDEXES

OPACs reference library print and nonprint holdings, including periodicals; however, they do not reference individual articles within newspapers, journals, or magazines. To access these types of materials, you need an index or online database.

Book Indexes

Like the OPAC, an index tells you the "address" or location of information within a specific resource. In nonfiction books, the index usually is located at the back of the book. A book's index is an alphabetical list of subjects referenced by page numbers showing where you can find that subject mentioned within the text. In a multivolume reference set, each volume may have its own index. In many cases, the index is a stand-alone index volume. Each subject in the alphabetical list in the index references the volume number and page number where the subject is mentioned in the resource.

For example, in a multivolume resource where the volumes are referenced by a separate index and volumes are separated alphabetically, "Abraham Lincoln" would be referenced as follows: Lincoln, Abraham L:259. The L is the volume letter and 259 is the page number where the article about Abraham Lincoln begins.

Some indexes use only numbers. For example, in a multivolume reference set where the volume is referenced by volume numbers, information on Abraham Lincoln would be referenced as follows: Lincoln, Abraham 10/259. The number on the left is the volume number. The number on the right is the page number where the article begins.

In many cases, Abraham Lincoln is discussed in multiple places. Additional references would be listed after the main subject listing, indented.

Lincoln, Abraham L:259
Booth, John Wilkes B:300
Gettysburg Address G:128
Grant, Ulysses S. G:238

Periodical Indexes

A periodical index is a cumulative list of articles from a set of periodicals arranged in alphabetical order by author, title, or subject, and typically within a specified date range. The entries or citations provide all the information needed to find a specific article.

An important difference between a library's catalog or OPAC and a periodical index is that a periodical index does not reflect the specific periodicals to which a specific library subscribes. Periodical indexes are published by commercial entities and index a preestablished set of periodicals whether a specific library does or does not subscribe to all of the periodicals referenced in the index. Once you find an article you want to read in a periodical index, you have to check the OPAC of the library you are in to see if the library actually subscribes to that periodical. If so, you can go to the periodical area of the library, locate the periodical and specific volume, and read the article.

Typically, periodicals cannot be checked out of the library; however, you can make a photocopy of the article—if you adhere to copyright restrictions. In larger libraries, periodicals often are separated by current (periodicals recently received) and bound (periodicals bound together by volume or by time period). Older periodicals may even be in a different place entirely in the library, such as in the basement, as they are not used often and can take up a lot of space.

HINT: Carefully read the signs posted in your library to see where the periodicals are located and how they are organized.

If the library does not subscribe to the periodical you need, you have three options:

1. Find a library that does subscribe to the periodical, and go there physically and read or copy the article.
2. Request that a copy of the article be sent to the home library through the library's interlibrary loan system. This usually involves a fee of a few dollars per page for copying and often takes a few days to receive.

3. Access the article electronically using a full-text resource available either through the library or on the Internet. To find the article electronically, use an electronic version of the periodical index. Clicking on the title of the article typically brings up the full text of the article, if it is available. In many cases, the abstract, or short summary, of the article can be read, even if the full-text version is not available. Many online resources provide full-text articles either without charge or for a single-use or subscription fee.

Thousands of periodicals indexes cover more than 150,000 individual periodicals. Before you can begin searching for an article, you must find the appropriate index in which to search. **General indexes** cover a broad range of topics in scholarly journals, popular magazines, and newspapers. **Subject-specific periodical indexes** cover articles in selected scholarly journals related to a broad topic or subject area. As examples, the *Business Periodicals Index* references articles in the business

CRITICAL THINKING QUESTIONS

Select a topic that you might want to research for one of your classes or for your career. Answer the following questions:

- In what subject area does my topic belong? (e.g., art, education, business, science)
- Do I need articles from professional journals or from popular magazines?
- Should I include both primary and secondary resources? Which would be best for my topic?
- Will my topic be covered in a general index, or should I look in subject-specific indexes?
- What indexes cover my subject or topic, and are they available at my library? In print? Electronically?
- How current does my information have to be?
- What indexes cover the necessary time periods?

step-by-step instruction

STEP-BY-STEP: USING A PERIODICAL INDEX

Step 1: Develop a list of keywords and subject headings for your topic.

Step 2: Determine the specific periodical index to use.

Step 3: Use the search word list and periodical index to find the exact citation for the article you want to read.

- Read the introductory material in a printed periodical index to see exactly how to use the periodical.
- Use the search tool in an electronic index and Boolean operators to narrow or broaden your search as needed.

Step 4: Go to the location in the library for the periodicals and use the title of the periodical, the volume and page numbers listed in the citation, and the actual title of the article to find the article you want to read.

Step 5: Make a copy of the article, if needed.

If your library does not subscribe to the periodical you need, use the interlibrary loan system to have a copy of the article sent to your library.

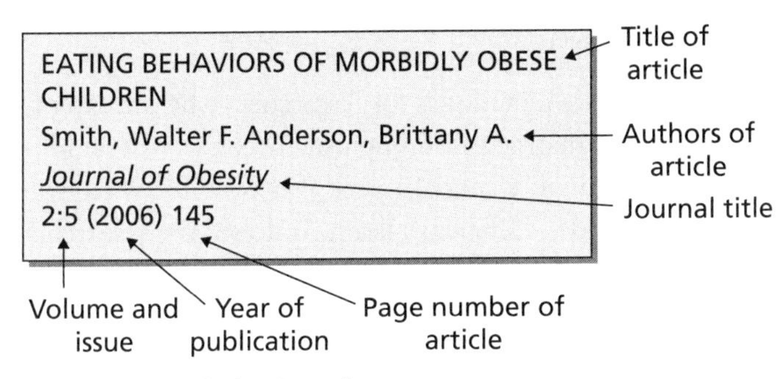

Figure 3-12 Citation Example

arena and the *Index to Legal Periodicals* references legal-related articles. To find the most appropriate periodical index for your area of research, consult with your librarian. Figure 3-12 shows an example of a citation and the information you need to find the article in the actual periodical.

DATABASES

A database is a collection of digitized information organized for simplified, fast searching and retrieval. Like an OPAC, databases can be searched by subject, author, title, and keyword. Boolean operators typically can be utilized with databases, too, to broaden or narrow a search. A database may contain just a citation, or a citation and abstract, or a citation and full-text article that includes the abstract. When you are searching in a database, you can limit your search in numerous ways, including searching by the type of publication, by the date of the publication, by the publication itself, and so forth. You can print portions of a database, save the database to be accessed later, or e-mail the database.

INFORMATION COLLECTION

Once you have developed your search statement and research questions, determined where you are going to find the information, and accessed the information, the next step is to collect the information from the information source. You can use several methods to collect your information.

3

SCANNING AND SKIMMING

Scanning and **skimming** are techniques for researchers who are exploring or seeking specific information. Scanning usually comes first and involves quickly moving through material to see if it contains what you need. If the scanning provides sufficient reason to do so, the researcher can go back and skim the information further. Use both scanning and skimming when you want to determine if an article is relevant to your research. Both scanning and skimming are good techniques when you have a lot of material to cover in a short time or if you have a lot of information to consolidate into a manageable amount.

Scanning is used to search for headings, keywords, ideas, or a specific piece of information. This technique is used when you know exactly what you are looking for and are concentrating on finding specific information. For example, when you are looking for a number or a name in a telephone book, you are scanning.

Skimming typically follows scanning but is equally important. Skimming is used to quickly determine the main idea in text by reading subheadings and the first sentences of sections and paragraphs. It allows the researcher to cover a great deal of information quickly and efficiently. It also gives the researcher an opportunity to determine whether a more in-depth reading is necessary.

To skim through a document, follow these tips:

- Read the first and last paragraphs of the text.
- Read the titles, headings, and subheadings within the text.
- Read the first sentence of each paragraph.
- Look for names, dates, and places.
- Review elements such as graphs, tables, charts, diagrams, and captions.
- Look for other organizational clues such as italicized words, bold print, and bulleted lists.
- Read any questions that may appear at the end of a text.

REFLECTION QUESTIONS

Select a chapter of a textbook that you are required to read for class in the next day or so. Scan the chapter, then skim the chapter. Then read the chapter fully.

1. How much information do you think you got out of the chapter before you read it fully?
2. Do you think that the scanning and skimming helped in comprehending the information?

HIGHLIGHTING

Highlighting is a technique that researchers use to mark important words, phrases, or passages of text for future use. Highlighting also can be used to discriminate between important information and interesting information. Important information is that which answers initial research questions or solves initial problems. Interesting information is that which the author uses to clarify the main points. As a researcher, you must be able to discern between the two types of information and not be distracted by extraneous text. Excessive highlighting minimizes its effectiveness by obscuring the main ideas, so you should highlight only major concepts and key phrases.

NOTE-TAKING

Note-taking is a technique that researchers use to organize and abbreviate highlighted or other collected information. The facts must be written as paraphrases or restated, not copied. Direct quotes must be given proper credit to avoid **plagiarism**—presenting someone else's ideas or words as your own. For each group of notes, include the source of the information. Recording your sources accurately and promptly simplifies the process and ensures that all of your sources receive proper credit. It is useful when citing (creating a reference list) the sources used in research. Citing references is discussed in more depth in chapter 6.

Some researchers use note cards for this purpose. Others prefer to use a computer or other graphic organizer. Notes are used to put together the final paper or project. Finding a method of taking notes with which you are comfortable will serve you throughout your life.

When taking notes, the following are key points:

- Categorize or separate each fact or phrase according to the main idea.
- Note the date you retrieved the information if the information is from an online source.
- Include the source of the information on each note card or in each section.
- Include on each note card or section the question or problem to be solved. Remember to constantly refer back to your search statement and research questions.
- Number each note card or section so you can keep the notes in order.

REFLECTION QUESTIONS

1. What is your current procedure for taking notes on the information you find in your research?
2. How effective do you think your note-taking strategy is?
3. What could you do differently to improve your note-taking effectiveness?

- Use abbreviations whenever possible, and consistently.
- Label each note card or section with the topic.

PHOTOCOPYING

You can photocopy the information you need in a library rather than checking out the resource and taking it home. You must photocopy articles in periodicals because usually you cannot check out periodicals from the library. In many libraries, the library staff will make photocopies for you and you will be charged a fee for each photocopied page. In other libraries, self-service photocopiers are available to library users. These copiers typically require change or a refillable money card purchased from the reference desk or circulation desk. Documents on microform also may be printed and copied.

At the beginning of this chapter, Danielle was given an assignment to write a research paper on a topic of her choice. By understanding the search and information retrieval process, she can be more efficient in finding and using information. Having an information-collection method in place will help keep her organized until she is ready to put together the final paper.

learning activities

Activity #1 Reviewing and Revising the Search Process

Select or create a research project. Use the Research Skills Worksheet as a road map for research or problem solving. Write down your response in the spaces provided. Then answer the following questions:

1. How did following this process help you find and access the information you needed?
2. As a result, do you think you were more efficient in your research?
3. What are the most difficult steps in this process? Why?

Research Skills Worksheet

Research Process	Task	Your Response
What is the problem or question to be addressed?	Write out clearly the specific assignment.	
What is the topic to be researched?	Write down your specific search statement.	
What questions have to be answered?	Write four research questions to accompany search statement.	
What key concepts have to be addressed?	Identify and write down two or three key concepts.	
What synonyms can be used for key concepts?	Write four to eight synonyms for key concepts.	
What perspective should be used to address the questions?	Determine the point of view—subjective, objective, multiple perspectives.	
How current does your information have to be?	Look at the questions and decide the importance of currency of the resource.	
What resources should be utilized?	List four to six specific resources to be used.	
Where are these resources located and accessed?	Write down call numbers for print resources, and access procedures for electronic resources.	
What means of information collection will be used?	Determine note-taking style, and record information.	
What information is needed to cite these sources?	Record the needed information for each source.	

Activity #2 Searching Practice: Part 1

Use the topic "computer literacy in the classroom" and a search engine on the Internet (www.google.com or www.yahoo.com) to practice searching for appropriate information.

1. What keywords should you use for this topic?
2. What are some synonyms for the keywords?

Type in the words or phrases, and examine your results.

3. What words or phrases might you not want to include in your keywords?
4. How can you combine your search terms using Boolean operators to narrow or broaden your results?

Activity #3 Searching Practice: Part 2

Using the OPAC, find one *book* on a topic related to this class.

Title: ______________________________

Author: ____________________ Call Number: __________

Will this be a good source for the topic? Why or why not?

Find one article from a scholarly journal on the topic, using a periodical index.

Article Title: ______________________________

Author: ____________________ Publication Date: __________

Periodical Title: ______________________________

Periodical Index Utilized: ______________________________

Will this be a good source for the topic? Why or why not?

LEARNING OBJECTIVES REVISITED

Review the learning objectives for this chapter and rate your level of achievement for each objective using the rating scale provided. For each objective on which you do not rate yourself as a 3, outline a plan of action that you will implement to fully achieve the objective. Include a timeframe for this plan.

	1	2	3
Use several techniques to efficiently search for relevant information	☐	☐	☐
Identify several common sources for information.	☐	☐	☐
Use library resources to find and access information.	☐	☐	☐
Explain the importance of having a method for collecting information	☐	☐	☐

Steps to Achieve Unmet Objectives

Steps	Due Date
1. ____________________	__________
2. ____________________	__________
3. ____________________	__________
4. ____________________	__________

3

POTENTIAL ITEMS FOR LEARNING PORTFOLIO

Refer to the "Developing Portfolios" section at the front of this textbook for more information on learning portfolios. Consider adding the following results from this chapter's learning activities or even ideas of your own to your learning portfolio.

- Completed Research Skills Worksheet

REFERENCES

Billington, J.H. (n.d.). *Welcome message from the librarian of Congress.* Retrieved September 5, 2006 from http://www.loc.gov/about/

Online Computer Library Center (2006). About DDC: Dewey Decimal Classification System. Retrieved September 5, 2006 from http://www.oclc.org/dewey/about/default.htm

CHAPTER OUTLINE

4 Evaluating Information

THE BIG PICTURE

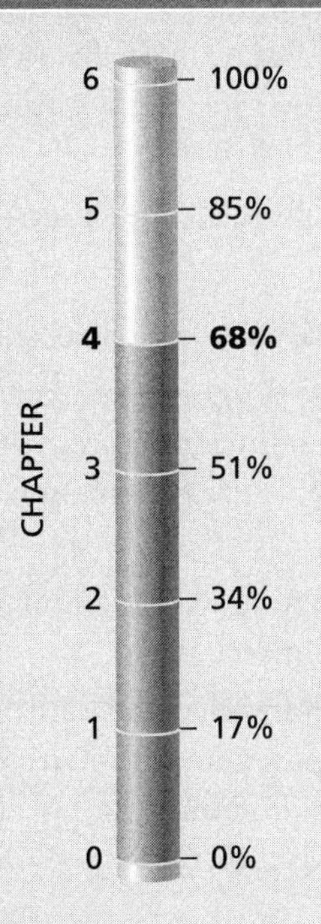

LEARNING OBJECTIVES

By the end of this chapter, students will achieve the following objectives:

- Use a set of criteria to evaluate information and information sources.
- Identify specific criteria that should be used to evaluate web pages for credibility and appropriateness.

©2007 JupiterImages Corporation

Selecting information that is accurate and credible is sometimes a challenge.

4

CHAPTER 4 SCENARIO

Finding information does not have to be a problem in the Information Age if you know where to look. Information and data abound in both print and electronic formats. Selecting information that is accurate and from credible sources presents a greater challenge. Consider the following scenario illustrating a situation in which effective evaluation of information is critical.

Sheryl Fraser is a medical assistant working for a large physician practice. Her supervisor has asked her to develop some nutrition pamphlets to hand out to patients, encouraging them to change poor eating behaviors in favor of a diet within recommended dietary guidelines. The nutrition books in the office are outdated, so Sheryl decides to seek the needed information on the Internet. She types the search term "nutrition" using the www.google.com search engine—which indicates about 243,000,000 websites. As she looks through the first few sites, she finds contradictory information. One site suggests eating a 10-day diet of grapefruit to lose weight fast. Another site recommends a high-protein, low-carbohydrate diet. A third site informs her that the only way to be healthy is to avoid all meat and dairy products and to adhere to a vegetarian diet. Though Sheryl did learn basic nutrition principles in her training as a medical assistant, she wants to be able to refer to credible resources to support the information in her pamphlet.

Imagine yourself in Sheryl's place. Thoughtfully and honestly answer the following questions:

- How will you begin to sort through the vast number of websites devoted to nutrition?
- Realizing the contradictory information on nutrition presented on the Internet, how will you determine which information is credible and which is not?
- How well do you think you will be able to judge which information you find is accurate and which is inaccurate?
- Do you think you will be able to successfully select the kinds of resources that will be appropriate to support your information? If so, on what criteria will you base your selection? If not, what do you need to know to make an effective choice?

- How will you find data you can translate into information that your patients will understand, knowing that most of your patients have limited backgrounds in health-related topics, especially nutrition?

THE IMPORTANCE OF CRITICAL ANALYSIS

Information-literate individuals critically analyze information and its sources to ensure that it is useful. Lack of critical analysis increases the risk of using inaccurate and inappropriate information, making poor decisions based on poor information, and losing time. Critical analysis applies to print materials and resources, multimedia resources, and information on the Internet. This chapter suggests several criteria you can use to analyze information and information sources as the next step in the research process. We will look first at criteria that can be applied to all information (books, articles, and websites) and then discuss tips that apply specifically to critiquing information found on the Internet. After you read this chapter, you should be able to apply critical analysis in asking questions about information sources, as well as provide criteria for evaluating information sources.

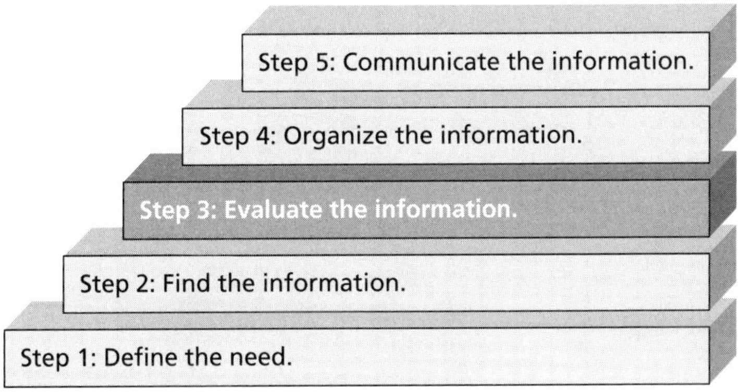

Step 5: Communicate the information.
Step 4: Organize the information.
Step 3: Evaluate the information.
Step 2: Find the information.
Step 1: Define the need.

Research Process Step 3: Evaluate the Information

The third step of any research project should be to critically evaluate the information found.

EVALUATING THE RESOURCE

Evaluating information is based in large part on common sense. Still, to understand evaluation criteria, it helps to understand how information is published and communicated.

PUBLICATION TIMELINE

The timeline for publishing information influences the content and defines how the information can be used effectively. Thus, the publication timeline becomes one of the criteria for evaluation. When an event occurs, radio and news agencies such as CNN may be able, via satellite systems, to give live reports of the event. Newspapers and magazines, however, take much longer to report the facts of the same event. You may read the facts in a newspaper by the next day's edition, but a magazine may take weeks or even months to publish the report. The timeline for publication of information in scholarly journals and books is even longer, because the processes are more complex and, in the former case, entail many steps in review. Large-volume resources, such as encyclopedias, directories, and handbooks may not publish the information for many months, if not years. Even though Internet technology allows almost instantaneous publication of the information, a real person must be updating the website constantly. Other than news websites, the information on the Internet is outdated quickly. Figure 4-1 provides a general timeline of information currency.

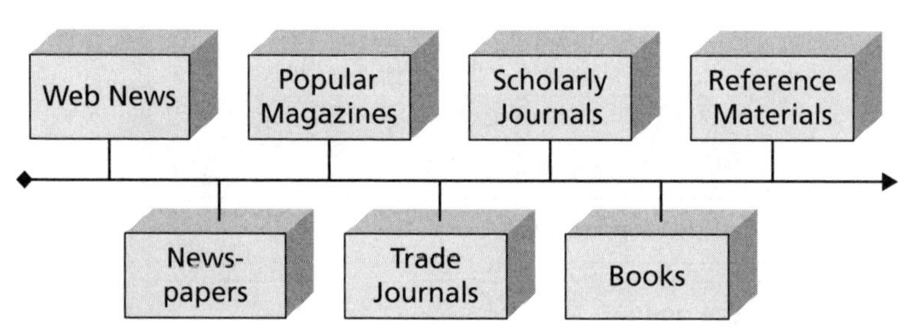

Figure 4-1 The publication time is dramatically different for different types of publications.

Different kinds of information are needed for different purposes. Following are examples of the best formats for various types of information, based on information flow and timing.

- *History.* History is an example of a topic that does not necessarily require up-to-the minute information. For some information projects, understanding historical facts is important. For example, if you are writing a report about an event in history, understanding the context in which that event occurred might be critical to the effectiveness of your finished project. You might want to know about the geographical area, the society and its culture, the political environment, the time period, and the area's demographics. Because this information does not change from the past and does not change quickly, a book or an encyclopedia might be an excellent source of the information. Historical sites on the Internet would provide the same type of information.
- *Technology.* Technology provides an example opposite that of history. Because changes in technology occur rapidly, the information a book contains about a given technology is likely to be outdated by the time the book is published. Take the example of a book describing a computer software program. An updated version of the software is likely to be available by the time the book is published. A better resource for this type of information would be a help manual published with the software or documentation from the website of the company that publishes the software.
- *Behind-the-scenes information.* In some cases, it is important to understand what occurred just before an event. This kind of information may be in the form of personal correspondence (e.g., memos, e-mails, letters, listservs), various types of documentation (e.g., diaries, journals, logs, personal notes, lab notes of an experiment), and other media (e.g., newsletters, conference programs). This information is not always easy to find or access, but it can help to explain why an event occurred or to document the chronology of events.
- *Immediate information.* Live news information sources, such as the Internet, provide immediate information. In many cases,

4

the facts of the event (who, what, when, how) are provided but the background or "why" of the event often is not yet known. This kind of information has to be critiqued carefully, as live reporting may be inaccurate when there is little time to check the facts.

- *Current information.* Current information includes information that is reported a few hours to a few days after an event. TV and radio reporting, newspaper reporting, and Internet reporting all provide this type of information. There may have been time to research the background of the event and to check the facts. The content may also include analysis, statistics, interviews, historical context, and other relevant information.
- *Older information (weeks).* Magazines provide information several days to weeks after an event. Because these information sources take time to publish the content, they allow sufficient time to check facts, research the background and historical context, find supporting data, conduct interviews, and enhance the information. Often these information sources report for a specific purpose, so the content must be critiqued for bias or a specific slant. The information is less current than live or next-day reports, and although there is time to check facts, accuracy is not guaranteed.
- *Older information (months to years).* Information that is several months, or even years, old is published in scholarly journals, conference papers, research reports, and books. These information sources require time to conduct detailed studies or analyses of data or events, review by peers or editors, and physical publication of the resources. Journals and conference papers that are found online adhere to the same process, so the time requirement is similar. An advantage is that these resources can provide more detailed, thorough, and accurate information.
- *Older information (years).* Information that is several years old typically is published in book form. It takes months to years to research and write a book, and additional time for its review, editing, and production. This type of resource can provide accurate and detailed information with supporting background, analysis, and commentary. Typically, books provide much more

information. They can support one perspective or provide numerous viewpoints. Currency of the information is sacrificed for volume and depth.

- *Reference resources.* Publications such as encyclopedias, handbooks, and statistical compilations all provide factual and typically unbiased information. These information sources sacrifice currency for detail and accuracy. They require time to check the facts and ensure accuracy, compile the information, and publish the resource. Sometimes these kinds of resources can be found on the Internet, but, like online journals, they require the same amount of time for gathering and organizing the information, and additional time to input the data into a database.

Reflection Questions

1. Think about your academic or workplace information needs. When might you need each of the different types of information?
2. What is an example of a resource in your field of study for each type of information?

4

TYPES OF RESOURCES

Journals and magazines are common sources of information. The three basic types of journals and magazines are: (1) scholarly journals, (2) trade publications, and (3) popular magazines. Each of these types has a different purpose and target audience. Collectively, they hold a wealth of useful information, but it is important to recognize the differences among them to critically evaluate the appropriateness of their content.

Scholarly Journals

Scholarly journals are written by authorities in a topic area or field of study and include research reports and other academic or factual information. The main purpose of a scholarly journal is to report original, current research data to individuals in the scholarly and professional arenas. Scholarly research means that scientists and researchers have conducted highly structured studies using accepted methods and have made educated, justifiable conclusions about the results. These scientists and researchers typically work for educational institutions, such as colleges and universities, or for private research organizations, such as research labs, think tanks, hospitals, and nonprofit groups. In their articles, they use the language and technical terminology associated with the specific field. They also employ a structured format and follow accepted guidelines for studying a specific topic. The research results in **qualitative data,** which describes the characteristics or observations of something, or **quantitative data,** which measures something.

In many cases, the articles are sent out to reviewers who are specialists in the field. The reviewers critically analyze the information, methods, results, and conclusions that the authors have drawn. The reviewers make recommendations to the publisher that the manuscript be accepted, revised in some way, or rejected because of poor study design or invalid conclusions. The review provides expert appraisal, and although the review does not guarantee accuracy, it does provide a check on the content, adding to the information's credibility. Poor research or inaccurate content has less chance of being accepted for publication in a scholarly journal than in other, less structured types of journals or magazines. A journal that uses this review system is called a **refereed** journal and the review as **peer reviewed.** Journals that employ this level of review of their articles are highly credible.

Some examples of the many hundreds of scholarly journals are

- *Journal of the American Medical Association* (commonly called *JAMA*)
- *Journal of Geology*
- *Reviews of Modern Physics*
- *Journal of Infectious Disease*
- *Journal of Computer Information Systems*
- *Journal of International Business Studies*
- *Journal of Interior Design*
- *The American Professional Constructor*

Authors whose articles are published in scholarly journals are required to follow a structured format for organizing and publishing an article. Each scholarly journal has a set of guidelines informing authors how their manuscript should be submitted. These guidelines can be found in the journal itself or obtained from the publisher or the journal's website. Editors of the scholarly journal assess the quality and appropriateness of each article against these guidelines to determine appropriateness for publication.

CRITICAL THINKING QUESTIONS

1. What are five refereed journals that apply to your field of study? How do you know they are refereed? (Consider using www.google.com or another online search engine, or talk to your reference librarian, to find at least five examples that might be useful in your research activities. Many journals have websites describing their publications.)
2. What are five journals that are not refereed? How do you know they do not use a peer review process?

4

To illustrate how reviews and manuscript guidelines are used, consider the following examples: The *Journal of Nutrition Education and Behavior* sends to three reviewers a manuscript addressing the topic of food behavior. These reviewers might be university professors who teach in nutrition programs and who have completed research and published their own articles on a nutrition behavior topic. Other appropriate reviewers could be nutritionists who are familiar with food behaviors and psychologists who specialize in this area.

Regardless of their professional position, all reviewers are selected based on their expertise in nutrition behavior theories and the kinds of studies that have been completed in the past. The reviewers also have access to the journal's guidelines, so they are knowledgeable about how the manuscript should be organized. The reviewers know how sound behavior studies should be organized and how to objectively evaluate the assumptions and conclusions from the data. They have a high level of education and have had substantial training in the topic area and in research design.

As article reviewers, their goal is to critically and objectively evaluate the assumptions, methods, and conclusions to ensure that only sound information is published. The reviewers often make suggestions to the authors, who then have the opportunity to implement the suggestions and thereby improve the quality of the article before publication.

This peer review process is important to maintain the credibility of scientific investigation and reporting. A goal of scientific researchers is to publish articles about their research. Publishing an article lets the scientific community know what they are doing. The scientific community then reports the results of the study to the general population. Without publication, researchers' efforts go unrecognized and the information does not get implemented into daily life. If the researchers do not conduct sound research and use the data appropriately, their studies do not get published. The entire system provides an important check and balance for all of us.

A close look at the organization of a scholarly journal article and the purpose of each part of the article will help you develop your ability to gain useful information. A review of the *Guidelines for Authors* available for almost every scholarly journal will show that articles in these journals are required to be structured in a similar fashion. Most accounts of research are presented in a format similar to what is described next.

Abstract. An abstract is a brief synopsis of the article. In business proposals and other documents, the abstract is commonly called the **executive summary.** An abstract typically is limited to a specified length (e.g., 500 words) and must include the basic components or facts of the article. It provides the context and reasons for doing the study or writing the article. A good abstract explains briefly how the study was accomplished, identifies the major results, and states the conclusion. It also may state briefly why the study is important. Reading the abstract of a scholarly journal article before delving into the entire article can save a significant amount of time by revealing whether the information is appropriate for your purpose. If you determine that the article is appropriate, you then can read the article in its entirety for more details.

Key words: Many scholarly journals include a list of words that help to identify the main concepts in the article. These key words show how the article has been categorized in various search engines and library indexes. In the example of the behavior change article, key words might include: behavior change theory, nutrition behavior, eating behavior, weight loss, and obesity. These key words can be used to search for articles on similar topics in journal indexes and search engines.

Introduction. Most journal articles begin with an introduction explaining why the authors have conducted the study or written the article and why the information is important. For example, in our nutrition behavior article, the author may start with a brief discussion of obesity as a significant problem in the United States, caused by poor nutrition. Most introductions end in some kind of **purpose statement** or **thesis statement** for the article. These statements explicitly state the intent of the study or article. In formal scientific studies, the purpose statement is replaced by a **hypothesis,** in which the authors make a statement that they will attempt to support with the results of their specific study.

Literature review. The **literature review** comes after the introduction and provides a brief overview of the relevant studies or articles that support or provide background information on the current study. The purpose of the literature review is to provide a solid foundation for the topic, using published information. One of the goals of scientific research is to add to the scientific body of knowledge in the field. Demonstrating the relationship of the current study to existing research clarifies that correlation and summarizes the scientific body of knowledge that relates specifically to the topic of the current study. The author must objectively review highlights, relevant findings, issues, controversies, successes, or failures of previous research.

For example, in the behavior change article, a thorough and informative literature review would highlight several behavior change theories or studies, including those that did not succeed. The author would be careful not to skew the perception to support the purpose of the study. Excellent literature reviews start out with a broad scope, then narrow the focus to point specifically to the need for the current study or article.

Some articles are written for the sole purpose of discussing the previous literature. These are called **review articles.** In the nutrition behavior example, a review article might highlight the major nutrition behavior theories studied in the past. Review articles do not include a methods section or a results section as described next. The review article is an excellent starting place for researching a scientific topic.

Methods. After the context and need for the study have been discussed in the introduction and the highlights from relevant previous studies have been summarized, the author explains in detail how the current study was conducted. Sound research methods contribute to the validity and reliability of the study. In addition, if another researcher wants to re-create the study, he or she could follow the methods described in the article. The description of the methods also allows the article's reviewers to determine if the study was conducted in a logical manner and if sound research standards and procedures were followed. If a tool, such as a questionnaire, was used, it should be included as an **exhibit** glossary at the end of the article. If it is not included, readers should be able to contact the authors to gain access to the tool that was used.

Results. The results section logically follows the methods section. Here, the author presents the results of the study in an objective, logical manner. Visual representations of data, such as tables, charts, graphs, diagrams, or photographs, are used frequently to illustrate the information. Establishing a direct correlation between the methods section and the results is vital to the study's credibility. The charts or tables should be labeled clearly and organized so readers can easily understand what is being communicated without reading the text of the article. Presenting information graphically whenever possible and appropriate adds to the clarity of the information.

Discussion. The next section in the article is a discussion of the results. Here, the author explains the results, discusses any problems that arose during the study that might have influenced the results, presents any unexpected event or finding, and relates the results back to the original findings in the literature. In some cases, the findings are supported by the literature review. In other cases, the findings contradict previous findings. In the event of a discrepancy, the author typically provides an explanation of the contradiction to the best of his or her ability. In most cases, the author makes an educated assumption about the findings, regardless of whether the findings supported or contradicted previous research.

Conclusions: Finally, the conclusions section explains the major inferences that can be logically drawn from the study and outlines why the findings are important to the industry or the general population. Authors often make recommendations for future research, including other topics that can be studied formally to help answer the research question or expand on the findings. A conclusion must be supported directly by results of the study versus the author's opinion.

References: Authors of articles in scholarly journals are required to state in their articles exactly where they get any information or facts. The source of a fact is indicated in the text of the article where the fact occurs and is called a **citation.** The complete source for the citation is provided in the **reference list** at the end of the article. Each journal provides its own **style guide,** including, among other requirements, specifically how to cite sources. Information on style guides is presented in chapter 6.

Citing references appropriately credits authors of original work and is essential to avoid **plagiarism** (stealing information or ideas from others). Plagiarism is highly unethical, illegal, and can lead to being reprimanded, fired, or sued. Using information that has been verified by others is acceptable and necessary to substantiate new research, but the original author or source of the information must be given proper credit.

Trade Publications

Trade publications (sometimes called trade journals) can be excellent sources of information, but they must be viewed critically for accuracy, credibility, and appropriateness. Authors of trade publications typically are specialists or practitioners in a given field. They write their articles for others in the same industry who face the same issues and have the same informational needs. Most information in trade publications is practical in nature, reporting on issues such as procedures, materials, technology, equipment, events, and policies or processes.

Typically, trade publications have no formal review process other than the basic editorial review, which ensures that the article is well-written and does not contain grammatical and typographical errors. In these publications, authors use the technical language of the field because the article is written for other industry professionals. Information is presented in charts, graphs, diagrams, and photographs, as appropriate. Although the authors often mention where they acquired their information, they generally do not cite their resources formally, which makes it difficult to find the original or primary source of the information.

A few examples of the many hundreds of trade publications are

- *Advertising Marketing and Research Reports*
- *Industrial Equipment News*
- *Concrete Products*
- *Building Design and Construction*
- *Business Solutions*
- *Computer Graphics World*
- *Veterinary Practice News*
- *Hospitality Technology*

CRITICAL THINKING QUESTIONS

1. What trade publications are available in your field?
2. How can you use the information from these types of publications appropriately?

Popular Magazines

Popular magazines are the least useful type of journal/magazine for credible research. The main purpose of the articles in popular magazines is to get readers to purchase the magazine or perhaps to sway the reader to a specific way of thinking or point of view. Authors of the articles in popular magazines are writers on staff with the magazine and rarely are specialists in the topic area. In addition, freelance writers, who typically are not specialists in any one area, sell their articles to the magazine for a fee. Freelance writers conduct research and interviews to find the information needed for a specific article. They are writers, not authorities. Their goal is to entertain or inform the general population, resulting in increased sales and profits for the publication.

The language of the article is typically less technical, as the target audience is usually the general public. As is the situation with trade journals, there is no review process other than the editorial review to ensure that the articles are well-written and free of grammatical and typographical errors. Even though some authors mention their sources of information, they rarely cite these sources formally, as required in a scholarly journal. Often, numerous photographs are used instead of the charts and graphs presenting quantitative data.

You should be cautious in using information from popular magazines. There is no guarantee that the information is accurate, unbiased, or appropriate, and it can be difficult to verify facts or find the original or primary source of information without formal resource citations. Still, popular magazines are useful in some areas of research and for some types of information. For example, an interior designer can use popular magazines to keep up with current and geographical trends in design, materials, and techniques. Popular magazines also commonly use interviews with leaders in the field, provide current news and discussion of issues, and follow market issues.

A few examples of the hundreds of popular magazines are

- *Men's Health*
- *Science and Nature*
- *Muscle and Fitness*
- *Entrepreneur Magazine*
- *Popular Science*
- *Wired*
- *PC Magazine*
- *Computer Gaming World*
- *Scientific American*
- *Psychology Today*
- *US News and World Report*

CRITICAL THINKING QUESTIONS

1. What popular magazines publish information related to your field?
2. How can you use the information from these popular magazines appropriately?

questions to ask

- When did the actual event occur?
- How current is the information in your source?
- How much time is required to transfer the information into the format of this resource?
- What kind of information is needed? What is the purpose of the information?
- How current should the information be?
- What is the best source of information based on the publication's timeframe?
- Do you have to find the original or primary sources of information?
- What is the purpose of the publication you are using for your research?
- Has the publication put its articles through a formal peer review?

EVALUATING AUTHORITY

After determining the kind of resource you want to use, the next step in evaluating your information is to determine the authority of its author. Evaluating the authority means to look critically at the author of the information as well as the sponsor or owner of the specific resource, such as the publisher or owner of a website. Your goal is to determine if those who write the information are qualified to do so and whether they are providing credible information. Several elements have to be evaluated when considering the author, publisher, and sponsor or owner of a website.

AUTHOR

In many information sources, the author's name is displayed prominently—on the front and title page of a book, on the first page of journal articles, and as a byline of newspaper and magazine articles.

In other resources, such as websites, finding the author may take a bit more effort. Some information sources, such as encyclopedias and reference materials, have a number of authors, as well as a group of contributors or an editorial board that oversees the information submitted.

Recall that a website is created for a specific purpose. For example, some websites sell products or services. Others convey information on a narrow topic area. Others attempt to persuade readers to a specific viewpoint or opinion. Still other sites are intended for entertainment. Some web pages are even created to cause damage to another individual or group. With this in mind, you can gain a great deal of information on the credibility of a website by evaluating the authorship or the person or organization that created and maintains the site. You must think critically about the purpose of the site. Holding the author or owner of a website to the same standard as that of an author of a printed document is important to credibility.

CRITICAL THINKING QUESTIONS

1. Conduct an Internet search for a topic in your field of study. What is an example of a website that has each of the following goals?
   - Selling a product or service
   - Informing readers of objective facts
   - Persuading readers to a specific way of thinking or supporting one side of an issue
2. How did you determine the goal of each site?

In some cases, especially on reputable websites, information about the author is easily found on the website itself. Look for "Contact Us," "About," "Background," "Philosophy," "Who Am I," or "Biography" on the site. Most websites give names, addresses, phone numbers, or e-mails inviting you to contact the site's owner or administrator. The goal is to try to find someone who is responsible for the site in terms of the information and its accuracy.

Several clues will help you determine author's authority, which will give you an idea about the credibility of the information:

- *Expertise:* Look for signs that the author is an expert in the topic area and brings knowledge to the material. Expertise can come from academic degrees, work experience, previous publications, and extensive research. Consider conducting an Internet search using the author's name to find any organizations the author is associated with, other publications he or she has written, news stories about the author, or other references. For some fields, biographical references provide information about many experts in a variety of fields. For example:
  - *Contemporary Authors,* by Thomson-Gale Publishers, provides biographical and bibliographical information on fiction and nonfiction authors.

- Marquis *Who's Who* publishes biographical references in many different professional fields and geographical areas.

HINT: These biographical resources may help in a few fields but do not cover all areas of study. Also, these references may not list individuals with significant expertise.

- *Academic background and credentials.* Look for evidence that the author has a credible academic background and qualifications for writing on the topic. Self-proclaimed experts or those who are merely impassioned about a topic may not be qualified to write about it. In research, a credible author might have a Ph.D. (or at least a Master's degree) in a related field signifying that he or she conducts research or teaches in the area. In medically related areas, the author might be an M.D. or other medical professional with a qualified background pertaining to the topic.
- *Work-related or other experience.* In the business world, clues to credibility might be evident in work experience rather than academic credentials. Many credible websites have "Biography" sections listing the author's work-related experience. You also can conduct an Internet search to see if the author's name is associated with a company or professional organization. In most search engines, putting the name in quotes facilitates the search. For example, search for "Bob Smith" in www.google.com. The company or organization's website also can provide additional information about the author. If the author is a professor at a university, for example, you can find out past and current research topics, courses taught, and committees on which the author serves.
- *Licensure or certification.* In other areas, an author might have a license or certification in a specific area, such as an MCSE (Microsoft Certified Systems Engineer), meaning that he or she has passed an examination in Microsoft operating systems. If you find a credential and want to see if it is valid, conduct a

search using the credential name or letters to find the sponsoring organization and the explanation of the specific credential. Most organizations state exactly what the certified individual must know to gain and maintain certification and also may provide a list of currently certified individuals in a directory.

- *Affiliation*. Look for the author's affiliations, such as with academic institutions, professional organizations, governmental agencies, and other professional groups. Authors who are affiliated with recognized organizations tend to be more credible. In many fields of study, professionals are expected to maintain membership in professional organizations. Also, check the affiliation itself. For example, Texas International University and the American Heart Disease Association sound credible, but they are not real even though the names are similar to authentic and highly credible organizations. Research the organization if you are not familiar with it and its purpose.
- *Other publications*. In some cases it is useful to find out what other publications the author has produced or contributed to. A simple search using the author's full name in quotes on www.google.com may turn up additional publications. Books typically have an "About the Author" page or information on the book jacket that provides a list of the author's previous publications. Reputable authors also are often cited by other scholars.
- *Contact information*. In many publications, information about the author is available so you can contact the author either directly or through the publisher of the resource. Look for telephone numbers, mailing addresses, and e-mail addresses.

HINT: An e-mail address with no other information is not sufficient for assessing an author's credibility. Anyone can easily create an e-mail address. If this is the only piece of information available, consider e-mailing the author to see if you can obtain additional information.

CRITICAL THINKING QUESTIONS

1. Think about your field of study. What credentials would you expect for authors of credible information?
2. What academic background, work experience, academic degree, license, or affiliations would you expect? Why?

PUBLISHER

Another important component of authority is the **publisher** of the resource. The publisher is responsible for the actual publication or website in which the information is located. Resources can be published by a university press, a trade press, a governmental agency, a not-for-profit organization, a specialized press, or an individual. Academic print products often are published by university presses, which tend to be scholarly and highly reputable. These publishers put their materials through a formal and rigorous screening to ensure that they meet the standards and goals of the publishing organization. The content often undergoes a peer review, which gives it high credibility. Trade presses publish trade journals and magazines, which tend to be less formal in their review of information and typically do not require a peer review of their content.

Information published by a government agency is generally credible. For example, the U.S. Government Printing Office (GPO) publishes numerous materials designed to keep Americans informed about the activities of the three branches of government. You can find information published by the GPO at its website on the Internet. Among the numerous materials published by the GPO are, for example, the 9-11 Commission Report, the Budget of the United States Government, congressional bills, economic indicators, and MedLine. Just about anything you want to know about the government that is available to the public is found here.

Another type of publisher is the **subsidy publisher.** Also known as a **joint venture publisher** or **vanity press,** these publishers generally charge authors a fee to publish their work. In contrast to a traditional publisher, who accepts the risk of publication and ensures high-quality materials by providing editorial services and marketing or distribution of the product, the role of the subsidy publisher usually is limited to the actual production of a book. The editorial and marketing tasks are the author's responsibility. Products from joint venture publishers can be of excellent quality, and many well-received books have come from these publishers. As with any resource, however, you must assess the accuracy, quality, and credibility of the information.

CRITICAL THINKING QUESTIONS

1. Go to the US Government Printing Office at http://www.gpoaccess.gov Think carefully about your area of study. What are ten different information sources published by the Government Printing Office that you might find useful in your job or academic courses?
2. Who are the best known publishers of information in your area of study?

4

CRITICAL THINKING QUESTIONS

1. Visit the website of a joint venture publisher. What guidelines are required for publishing something?
2. What services does the publisher provide to the author?

REFLECTION QUESTIONS

1. Why would someone want to publish his or her materials through a subsidy press?
2. What advantages and disadvantages would this kind of publishing have?

SPONSOR OR OWNER

In addition to researching the author and publisher, you should investigate the sponsor or owner of the resource. This is especially important when assessing websites. A sponsor may be an organization or an individual. A large and reputable organization, such as the American Heart Association, tends to be more credible than an unknown individual. Determine if the sponsor advocates a specific viewpoint or philosophy. This information usually can be found in the "Home" or "About Us" section of a website or on promotional print materials.

On a website, in addition to "About Us" or "Home," look at the header or footer for a distinctive watermark or branding on the page to find information about the sponsor or owner. Try to determine if sponsors or owners are stable and durable, indicating that they are reliable and will be around for the long term. A large professional organization tends to be more stable and durable than an individual. A URL ending in .edu designates that the sponsorship is an academic institution. A URL ending in .gov indicates that the sponsor is a government agency. These sources tend to be more credible than commercial or organizational sites. Keep in mind that anyone can publish anything on the Internet and websites can be taken down at any time. Also, look to see if you can contact the webmaster of the site, and you can use www.whois.net to find information about the owner of the domain name for websites.

When evaluating sponsors, look carefully at *why* they are presenting the information. This question is important for print and Internet resources alike. Does the sponsor have a mission associated with the content? For example, the mission statement of the American Heart Association is to "reduce disability and death from cardiovascular diseases and stroke." (American Heart Association, 2006). You would expect credible information on health, disease, and related information from this association. Because it is a not-for-profit agency, it does not have the ulterior motive of selling products or making money from sponsoring this information. In contrast, a manufacturer of a health-care product is in the business of making money by selling that product. Therefore, information sponsored by this kind of organization should be evaluated more critically to determine the accuracy and credibility of the content.

HINT: Just because an entity sells a product or makes money from the information does not mean that the information is biased or inaccurate; it only means that you should check out the information carefully and keep in mind the purpose of the organization.

You can find just about anything you want on the Internet: scholarly resources, full-text documents, directories, virtual libraries, university websites, academic research, information portals, silly and joke sites, advertisements, trade sites and information, scams, personal pages, illegal activities, music, videos, and about anything else you can dream of. On the one hand, some of this information is excellent—reliable, verifiable, accurate, credible, and legal. On the other hand, much of the information on the Internet is not useful or appropriate—inaccurate, false, slanted, and sometimes illegal. Unfortunately, telling the difference from appearances alone can be difficult. The information-literate individual must know how to distinguish the good information from the bad. Train yourself to view web resources critically, even to the point of taking on a suspicious attitude toward each site you visit. This attitude will keep you critically analyzing the information that you find.

HINT: Do not accept everything you read just because it is found online. Anyone can write and post anything for any purpose on the Internet.

CRITICAL THINKING QUESTIONS

1. When researching information in your field, what kind of sponsor or owner would you expect to be credible? Why? Give some examples.
2. When researching information in your field, what kind of sponsor or owner would you be highly suspicious of? Why? Give some examples.

WEB ADDRESS

Some information found on a website gives clues about the author, publisher, and sponsor or owner. By understanding the clues, you can more readily make an informed decision about the quality of the information and the site itself. Figure 4-2 provides a fictitious URL—**Universal Resource Locator**—that serves as the example for the following discussion.

In our example, the top-level domain name is .edu, meaning that the server resides at an academic institution. The Internet Corporation for Assigned Names and Numbers (ICANN) is the entity responsible

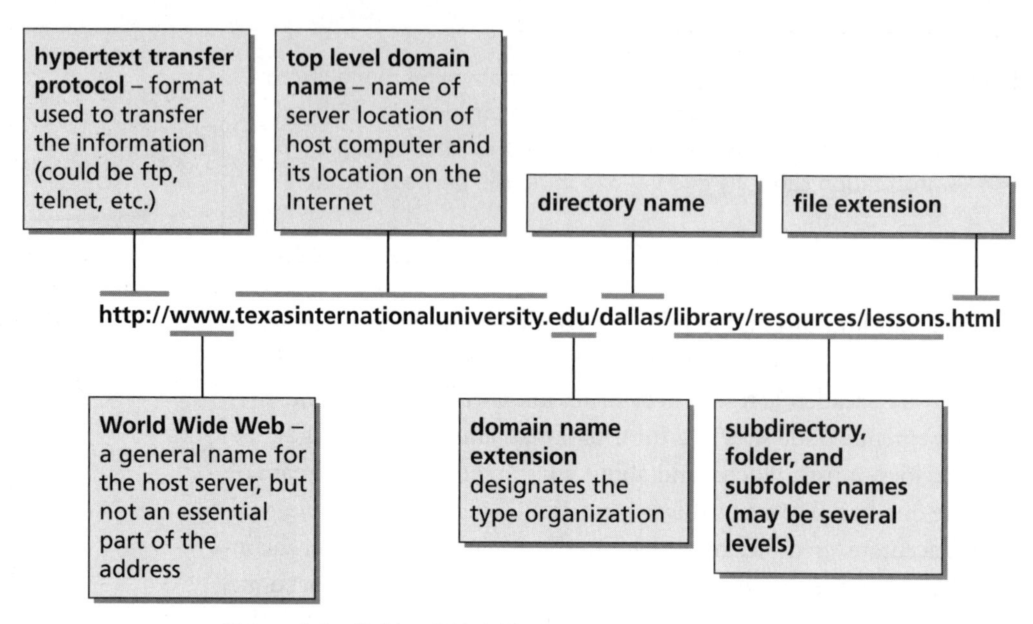

Figure 4-2 Fictitious Web Address

for approving these top-level domain names. Figure 4-3 provides a list of other common types of server locations that you should know.

Other extensions that currently are operational or may be operational and available for use soon include: .name, .travel, .pro, and .int. In addition, each country has its own two-letter code that often is used in conjunction with the top-level domain name. For a complete list of country codes, go to the International Organization for Standardization (ISO) (www.iso.org). As examples, the ISO code for the United Kingdom is .uk and the ISO code for Botswana is .bw. When the ISO is used in the domain name, it signifies that the server is located in that country.

HINT: Typically, you can rely on the .gov and .edu sites as being reliable and presenting relatively accurate information. The government or educational entity behind the site usually is bound by a code of ethics and is watched by many different individuals or agencies. The other top-level domain name extensions do not afford the same level of confidence because these may have vested interests or may be created by individuals who have personal or organizational agendas.

Extension	Type of Organization	Description
.edu	Educational institution	The .edu extension tells that the website is sponsored by an educational institution, usually a college or university. These sites are often more reliable and credible than commercial or personal websites.
.com	Commercial organization	The .com extension tells that the website is a commercial site. These sites typically give information about a company, promote and advertise the company's products and services, and sometimes allow for online purchasing. The information is typically reliable, but is not scholarly.
.gov	Government agency	The .gov extension is reserved for governmental agencies and owned by the United States Federal Government. The information on these sites is typically viewed as credible.
.mil	Military entities	The .mil extension is reserved for military entities—Army, Navy, Air Force, Marines, and so forth.
.net	Internet service providers	The .net extension is sponsored by an Internet Service Provider.
.org	Organizations	The .org extension is reserved for organizations such as not-for-profit, religious, lobby, and charitable organizations. Information on these sites is typically credible; however, organizations exist for a purpose. Look carefully at the mission of the organization as you review the information.
.aero	Air transportation industry	The .aero extensions is newly authorized and is sponsored by the air transportation industry.
.biz	Businesses	The .biz extension is reserved for large and small businesses.
.coop	Cooperatives	The .coop extension is newly authorized and is sponsored by the National Cooperative Business Association (NCBA) for cooperatives.
.info	Information	The .info extension is sponsored by the Afilias Global Registry Services and developed for information sites.
.museum	Museums	The .museum is sponsored by the Museum Domain Management System and is reserved for museums.
~	Personal web page on a server	A "tilde" ~ often denotes a personal webpage on the server. In our example in Figure 4-2, adding /~BSmith after the .edu extension might signify a professor's personal website on this server. Review personal web pages carefully, as they may not be monitored as closely as pages created for institutions or departments of institutions.

Figure 4-3 URL Extensions Help Identify a Site's Sponsor

4

questions to ask

- Who is the author?
- What are the author's academic credentials related to the topic?
- What is the author's experience related to the topic?
- What kind of credential(s) does the author have (such as a license or certificate)?
- What is the author's affiliation?
- What else has the author published?
- Is the author well-known in the field?
- Is information provided so you can contact the author?
- Who is the publisher, and what kinds of materials are published?
- Who is the sponsor or owner (especially of websites), and is that sponsor stable?
- What is the sponsor's philosophy?
- Is the sponsor suitable to address this topic?
- Did the author prepare this information as a part of his or her professional duties or have some other relationship with the sponsor?
- What does the site's address tell you?
- If the site is from another country, is it valid for the purpose of your research?
- Does the top-level domain give you any clues about the credibility of the information?
- Is this someone's personal website?
- Where does the server reside? Does this make sense for the type of information found on the site?

EVALUATING CURRENCY

Currency refers to the timeliness of the information. On a print product, currency is determined by the date of publication. As you will recall, different types of publications require different timelines. Newspapers are published in a few hours after the event. Books can take months or even years to get the information into print, so the date of publication must be viewed in light of the type of information resource. Although web pages can take much less time to publish information, it is difficult sometimes to determine the currency of the information. An information-literate individual also understands how current the information has to be for the specific purpose. For some needs, the information must be as up-to-date as possible. For other purposes, such as historical research, currency is not important.

Additional clues can be found within the information itself. Look carefully at the references the author uses. A journal article that has been published recently but uses references from ten years ago is not likely to be as current as one that uses more recent references. In the scientific community, many changes and advancements can happen in a short time. Also, look for clearly dated information. For example, if the article refers to a statistic about computer use in public schools, check the date of the original source. If that statistic is from 1980, it is not relevant today.

DATE AND EDITION OF A PUBLICATION

In a print product, look for the copyright date on the reverse side of the title page. Determine if the date is appropriate for the topic. Many information sources are revised periodically, resulting in multiple editions. More than one edition indicates that the material has been updated to reflect new information and to correct mistakes. Multiple editions suggest a more reliable resource because the publisher chooses to continue to publish the book's subsequent versions.

DETERMINING CURRENCY OF A WEBSITE

On websites, the date of the last revision is often found on the bottom of the first page or on every page. A reputable website typically gives the last date the site was updated. In some cases, each page has a date, indicating the currency of the information. For example, if an organization's website has a page for the Board of Directors and the page has a current date, you can assume with some certainty that the information is current. Although not true in every case, a current date usually is an indicator of currency, but be aware that a site could indicate an update and still contain outdated information.

Obviously, not all information requires the same attention to currency. A website on the ancient history of Greece does not require the same currency as a site that provides the latest state regulations on Medicare and Medicaid. A site that provides state regulations on Medicare and Medicaid from 1987 is of little use except for historical reference. In some cases, you might want the information posted on the site near the time the incident actually occurred. News websites often archive their periodicals so you can see the stories as they were written at the time.

REFLECTION QUESTIONS

1. Think about a specific research project that you have had to do in school or in your job. How current did this information have to be?
2. For this project, what kinds of information sources would be best to use? Specifically, how would you determine the currency of the information?

WEBSITE STABILITY

Unlike a print product, a website can be changed in a moment and viewers may or may not be informed of the changes. The site can even be moved to a different address with no forwarding information, making it difficult to locate, or deleted from the Internet altogether. A good clue to determine the stability of the site typically lies in the sponsorship. A nationally recognized organization (e.g., American Red Cross), a governmental agency, or an academic institution (e.g., a college or university), or a large corporation (e.g., AT&T) probably is not going anywhere—at least not without making national news. The main websites usually can be relied upon to remain stable. The consequences of an established organization's moving its website can be significant. Conversely, an individual's personal website might move with little or no serious repercussions.

Keep in mind that a regular registration fee is required to maintain ownership of the web address, and some time and effort to maintain the site itself. Clues to websites that are not maintained include broken or dead links (links that do not go to the intended site on the Internet), outdated links (links that go to old information when it appears that they should be going to current information), and information that does not match other resources you have determined to be current.

CRITICAL THINKING QUESTIONS

1. Suppose an article you read suggests an information source from the Internet. You want to verify the facts by going to that information source but the web page had been discontinued. What will you do?
2. What will you want the author of that content to have done to help you in your research?

HINT: Although you cannot be guaranteed that a site is stable and will be there when you want to return to it, it is best to try to use information from relatively stable sources. When you cite your references in a document and someone wants to review your sources of information, you may run into difficulties if the site you have referenced is no longer accessible.

REFLECTION QUESTION

1. What kinds of issues might cause a website to be ignored or deleted from the Internet?

questions to ask

- How current does the information have to be?
- What is the date of publication of the resource?
- What is the edition of the resource?
- Can you determine how often the site is updated and when the last update was completed?
- Can you determine the currency of the original source of the information by looking at the references?
- Does the site seem like it will be there for a long time?
- Is the sponsoring organization stable, meaning that is it a viable organization that will probably be around for a while?
- Is the site sponsored by an individual who might soon tire of keeping up the site?
- Does the site receive sufficient attention, or has the author simply abandoned the site?

EVALUATING THE CONTENT

After you have evaluated the resource itself, the authority of the author of the content, and the currency, you will evaluate various aspects of the content itself. When looking critically at the content, you should evaluate for whom the material was written, purpose and scope of the information, objectivity of the information, and its accuracy and verifiability. Examining these characteristics in depth will illustrate their importance in the evaluation process.

©Digital Vision

INTENDED AUDIENCE

A first step is to determine the intended audience for whom the information was written. In general, information is written for specialists in the field, practitioners, a general audience or the general public, an educated audience, or some kind of specialized group. On the one hand, information that is highly technical is intended for clinicians, physicians, technicians, or practitioners. It may be too technical for laypersons or for an overview of a topic. On the other hand, information that is too general and is written for the general public may not be useful to a practitioner or researcher who requires detailed, technical information. The intended audience of the information and the information source dictate the type, depth, and focus of the content. In general, you should ask if the content is sufficiently scholarly to meet your goal but not so technical that it is too difficult to understand.

questions to ask

- Who is the intended audience?
- Is the tone and treatment of the information appropriate for the intended audience?
- Are the terms and concepts too technical to understand?
- Are the terms and concepts too simplified to be useful?
- Are the depth and detail sufficient for the needs of the audience?

REFLECTION QUESTIONS

1. Who are the various intended audiences for information in your field of study?
2. For each audience, what is the level and focus of the writing and content?

PURPOSE AND SCOPE

The next step is to look at the information to try to understand its **purpose.** Why was the information written or produced in the first place? Was the goal to inform, entertain, trick, sell, persuade, or damage? Some sources are created to provide new information; other sources are created to update existing information. In many cases, content is written so it provides only one side or view of an issue. Other resources provide a balanced treatment of all sides of an issue.

Scope refers to how broad or narrow the topic is. An overview topic typically is broad in scope, with few details. A narrowly focused treatment of the topic gives details on a small portion of a larger topic. This is why you have to thoroughly understand your need for the information, and then decide how in-depth the information has to be. For scholarly journals, review articles give an overview of the major findings of a topic. Each article referenced in the overview article follows with details on a narrow subtopic. In many research projects, broadly scoped sources are sufficient for describing the context or background of a topic. Then, more narrowly focused sources are used to detail the main topic of the project.

REFLECTION QUESTION

1. Think about a topic that you might research in your field of study. For the topic you select, what information would be considered background or an overview? What information would provide more focused details?

- What is the purpose of the information?
- Do you detect ulterior motives, such as selling, persuading, damaging, and so forth?
- Is the information a primary source or a secondary source?
- What is the scope of the information?

OBJECTIVITY

When evaluating content, you will have to determine whether information is fact or opinion. **Facts** are things that can be proven to have happened or to exist. **Opinions** are statements or judgments or beliefs, which may or may not be true. Facts should be backed up by a credible source and should be verifiable. You could go to a primary source to find the same information. Keep in mind, though, that opinions can be written to look like they are facts.

HINT: It is important to look at the facts the author provides as well as facts the author does not provide. For example, an author may provide accurate facts about the benefits of taking a specific medication for a disease but leave out the serious side effects of taking the medication.

Information is presented from a specific point of view. In a **neutral point of view,** only the facts are presented, without bias. **Bias** means that the facts are presented with prejudice. An information source should be critiqued to see if there is any prejudice or bias in the way it is presented. For example, if a health food store publishes a newsletter highlighting the benefits of taking the vitamins sold in the store but fails to discuss any research suggesting that taking the vitamins has no benefits or negative consequences, the newsletter has a biased point of view. Opinion pieces, commentaries, and book reviews are all written with a specific point of view.

Most news agencies are said to have one point of view or another (e.g., conservative or liberal). You will have to study the content to determine the point of view. Content should be evaluated based on whether the author conveys personal emotions or prejudices, makes unjustified claims or excessive claims of certainty, or distorts facts to support a point of view.

HINT: Biased information is not necessarily bad information, but it is important to recognize biased information and then seek out the opposite viewpoint so you will have a clear understanding of the entire issue or topic.

Many websites have host advertisements to support the website. Although the presence of advertising does not negate the credibility of the information, it should cause you to take notice. Evaluate the advertisements carefully to determine if the relationship with the products or services being advertised influences the objectivity of the information. On web pages, advertising should be clearly separate from objective material. Websites should be straightforward, clearly differentiating advertisements from objective facts or statements.

Tips for recognizing biased content:

- excessive claims of certainty
- appeal to emotion
- personal attacks
- too good to be true
- something for sale
- associated cost or fee
- unsupported claims of fact
- ignoring or omitting contradictory facts or views
- appeals to popular opinion
- before-and-after testimonials
- suggestive or negative innuendos

- magnification or minimization of problems
- presentation of information out of context
- sarcastic or angry tone
- advertisements

HINT: Credible scientists do not use the word "prove . . . Instead, they frame their findings as "the research suggests. . ." or "there is a correlation between. . . ."

- Is the information presented fairly and from a neutral point of view?
- Is there a specific motive for presenting the information?
- Are all sides of a story presented?
- Who is the author, and why is he or she presenting the information?
- What is the purpose of the information?
- Are facts and statements justified and backed up with sound research or primary sources?
- Is the author moderate or extreme in presenting the views?
- Is there a conflict of interest?
- If there is advertising, is it appropriate and separate from the objective information?

CRITICAL THINKING QUESTIONS

1. In your area of study, how might information-providers be biased? Give specific examples.
2. What are controversial topics or issues in your field about which authors might show emotion or have extreme views?

4

ACCURACY AND VERIFIABILITY

Along with objectivity, you will have to determine if the information is accurate and whether it can be verified with another credible resource. **Accuracy** covers a wide scope including

- accurate facts
- accurate reference to other resources

- no typographical errors
- no grammatical or punctuation errors
- logical assumptions
- logical flow of information
- logical conclusions based on information
- accurate visual aids, such as charts, graphs, and diagrams
- appropriate coverage of material

HINT: Look to see if the author can be contacted to verify facts or answer clarifying questions.

4

Verifiable means that the information is based on facts that can be authenticated by another credible source or several credible sources. The best information cites the original or primary resource. The resources have to be available for checking to ensure that they exist and actually support the statements and facts in the content. On a web page, check the links to see if they go to where they say they will go and if the linked source is also credible. For print references, consider checking the listed references to ensure that they support what has been stated. Also, compare the facts or statements made in one source with what is generally accepted.

For example, consumption of high-fat foods and lack of exercise are generally recognized as increasing the risk for heart disease. A resource that states otherwise goes against what is accepted to be true in the scientific community. Though new uses of technology and discoveries can result in changes to generally accepted ideas, these statements must be critically evaluated before accepting them.

HINT: If an information resource does not enable you to readily check the references, be suspicious of the information.

- What is the subject? Is it consistent with the title of the document or resource?
- Is the information free from grammatical, typographical, and punctuation errors?
- Are the assumptions, the flow of information, and the conclusions logical?
- Are the visual aids accurate?
- Are facts and statements justified and supported with sound research or primary sources?
- Can the references be verified?
- Do the statements agree with what is generally accepted as being true?
- Is the information complete, or are data missing that, if provided, might change the interpretation of the document or resource?
- For Internet information, is the information available in another format, such as a printed product in a library?

OVERALL QUALITY

In addition to accuracy of the information, the overall quality has to be evaluated, assessing the structure of the document and how the information is arranged. High-quality information is arranged in a logical and consistent manner. The information is broken down into logical sections or parts and is well laid out. Headings describe the content accurately. Visual aids, such as graphs, photos, charts, and tables, provide additional information and do not distract readers from the material. Visual aids are able to stand alone. You are able to understand the information from the graphic without requiring explanation from the text.

In addition to the actual content, copyright issues must have been addressed and dealt with legally and ethically. More will be said in chapter 6 about the ethical and legal issues surrounding information.

REFLECTION QUESTIONS

1. What impact does lack of editing (demonstrated by typographical and grammatical errors) have on the information you read?
2. What impact does an illogical arrangement of information have on the resources you use?

questions to ask 

- Is the information presented in a logical manner?
- Is the presentation consistent?
- Do the visual aids add to comprehension of the material?
- Can the visual aids stand alone?

success steps

STEPS IN EVALUATING INFORMATION AND INFORMATION RESOURCES

Step 1: Evaluate the resource.

Step 2: Evaluate the authority.

Step 3: Evaluate the currency.

Step 4: Evaluate the content.

- Intended audience
- Purpose and scope
- Objectivity
- Accuracy and verifiability
- Overall quality

EVALUATING MULTIMEDIA

So far, our focus has been on evaluating print and Internet resources. **Multimedia** resources include graphics, video resources, audio resources, simulations, animations, clip art, photographs, and software. These resources can provide important information in an interesting delivery format. As with print and Internet resources, however, this type of information must be evaluated critically to determine if it is appropriate, credible, and useful for your purposes.

All information should be evaluated in a similar way, regardless of how it is delivered or presented. Apply the same criteria as you would for a print or Internet resource:

1. Evaluate the resource.
2. Evaluate the authority.
3. Evaluate the currency of the resource and information.
4. Evaluate the content itself.

Additional criteria for evaluating multimedia resources include the following.

- **FUNCTIONALITY.** How well do multimedia work within the environment in which they are being viewed? For many multimedia choices, technical aspects determine how or if the information can be viewed. If viewing multimedia from a CD-Rom or DVD, the application should work without error on the computer. Multimedia viewed on the Internet should load relatively quickly and should clearly state if any additional plugins or software is needed for viewing. For Internet multimedia, viewers often are required to download a special application, such as QuickTime, Java, ActiveX, or Acrobat Reader. In most cases, these plugins are free and easily accessible on the Internet. A good website has a link to the pages where the software can be downloaded.
- **USABILITY.** Usability means that the multimedia are easy to use, or "user friendly." This criterion is especially important with software, animations, simulations, audio objects, and video objects. Layout should be logical and consistent throughout the object. The navigation should be intuitive and easy to find and follow. Any instructions should be clear and complete. Links should be functional, and if they are not, there should be a mechanism for reporting nonfunctional links to a Webmaster.

  Multimedia objects should download quickly, even at slower Internet speeds, and downloading instructions should be clear. If the tool is complicated, such as is the case with certain software, there should be a Help tool to answer common questions or provide instructions for all actions.
- **ACCESSIBILITY.** Many features make a multimedia object accessible to individuals who have various disabilities. An example

CRITICAL THINKING QUESTION

1. What kinds of multimedia might be useful in your field? Give several examples of multimedia you might be required to evaluate.

of a design feature of a web page is an ALT tag for links and images to assist sight-impaired viewers. A complete list of standards for accessible design can be found on the Americans With Disabilities website at www.ada.gov

4

success steps

STEPS IN EVALUATING MULTIMEDIA RESOURCES

Step 1: Evaluate the resource.

Step 2: Evaluate the authority.

Step 3: Evaluate the currency.

Step 4: Evaluate the content.

- Intended audience
- Purpose and scope
- Objectivity
- Accuracy and verifiability
- Overall quality

Step 5: Evaluate the functionality.

Step 6: Evaluate the usability.

Step 7: Evaluate the accessibility.

In the scenario presented at the beginning of this chapter, Sheryl Fraser had to develop some nutrition pamphlets to inform the patients in the clinic about sound nutrition behaviors. She realized that to provide accurate and credible information to her patients, she had to fully understand how to evaluate the information she found. Because the Internet was the most convenient way to find nutrition information, she realized that she had to pay particular attention to evaluating websites and the information they provided. Sheryl decided to use only government and academic websites for this project, to ensure that she was not misleading her patients in any way.

learning activities

Activity #1: Information Checklist

Goal: ***To review and organize the criteria for evaluating information and information sources and to create a checklist for this evaluation.***

STEP 1: Review the various criteria for evaluating information resources and the content.

STEP 2: Develop a checklist that will ensure that you complete a thorough evaluation when you conduct your research.

Activity #2: Information Resource Comparison

Goal: ***To emphasize the importance of understanding the type of resource and how to evaluate credibility and timing.***

STEP 1: Every person in the group should select one topic and then bring in one example of each of the following types of information sources:

a. a refereed scholarly journal

b. a trade publication

c. a popular magazine

STEP 2: Present your examples to the group and compare the characteristics of each that you would assess as you evaluate the resource.

Activity #3: Web Research

Goal: ***To develop a full understanding of the various kinds of information found on the Internet.***

STEP 1: Conduct an Internet search to find examples of the following types of websites:

d. an excellent web page that provides highly credible information

(continued)

4

e. a questionable web page that provides information for which you cannot easily determine the credibility

f. a web page designed to sell you something

g. a web page designed to influence your opinion on a controversial issue by using emotion and extreme remarks

h. a web page designed as a hoax or to purposely mislead the reader for some purpose

STEP 2: Print out a copy of each web page and clearly identify the characteristics that give you clues about the type of information the page provides.

LEARNING OBJECTIVES REVISITED

Review the learning objectives for this chapter and rate your level of achievement for each objective using the rating scale provided. For each objective on which you do not rate yourself as a 3, outline a plan of action that you will take to fully achieve the objective. Include a timeframe for this plan.

1 = did not successfully achieve objective

2 = understand what is needed, but need more study or practice

3 = achieved learning objective thoroughly

	1	2	3
Use a set of criteria to evaluate information and information sources.	☐	☐	☐
Identify specific criteria that should be used to evaluate web pages for credibility and appropriateness	☐	☐	☐

Steps to Achieve Unmet Objectives

Steps	Due Date
1. ____________________	__________
2. ____________________	__________
3. ____________________	__________
4. ____________________	__________

POTENTIAL ITEMS FOR LEARNING PORTFOLIO

Refer to the "Developing Portfolios" section at the front of this text for more information on learning portfolios. Consider adding the following results from this chapter's learning activities or even ideas of your own to your learning portfolio.

- Checklist for Evaluating an Information Resource and Information
- List of information resources that are useful in your field of study. categorized by type of resources

4

REFERENCE

American Heart Association (2006). *About us: Our mission.* Retrieved September 5, 2006, from http://www.americanheart.org/presenter.jhtml?identifier=1200029

CHAPTER OUTLINE

5 Organizing Information

THE BIG PICTURE

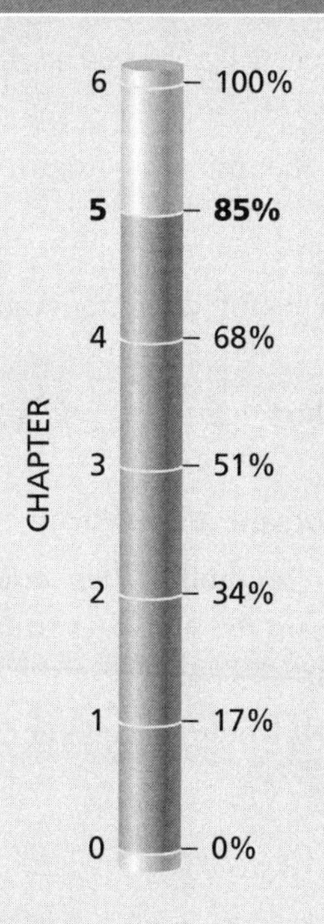

LEARNING OBJECTIVES

By the end of this chapter, students will achieve the following objectives:

- Explain the purpose and importance of effective information organization.
- Describe methods of organizing verbal and visual information.
- Select and apply an appropriate method for organizing information.
- Describe the uses of information and considerations when organizing information for each use.

CHAPTER 5 SCENARIO

Information must be organized logically to effectively communicate the intended message.

Information must be organized logically to communicate the intended message effectively. The following scenario illustrates a situation in which the organization of information is critical to completing a task successfully.

Anna Hensley graduated from college six months ago. Recently she accepted a position as a research assistant for a human resources firm, where her duties include accessing, organizing, and presenting information on hiring trends, salaries, industry growth, and other topics related to the human resources field. She also is responsible for preparing funding proposals for various projects. Anna must be able to locate relevant information, organize it logically into a document appropriate to her purpose, and present it effectively. During her orientation period she was guided by her supervisor's expertise. Now Anna has received the first major assignment that she is to complete independently. Although she is adept at locating and collecting information that supports her research goals, she is less sure of her ability to organize and present the information effectively. She is concerned about selecting the appropriate type of report or document, what information to include, how to organize it, and how to present it in a way that her audience will understand and that will achieve the project goals.

Imagine yourself in Anna's place. Answer the following questions thoughtfully and honestly:

- How familiar are you with various types of documents and reports and their uses?
- For each type of document or report, how logically could you organize the information?
- How would you go about selecting an organizational plan?
- How would you select your presentation method? When would you use a verbal format? When would you use a visual format? When would you consider other media?
- If you decide to use a table or chart, how would you present its content logically and clearly?

- If you select another presentation medium (such as Microsoft PowerPoint), what considerations would you make during preparation?

INFORMATION ORGANIZATION: AN OVERVIEW

Step 4 of the research process involves organization. Many elements contribute to effective organization of information. The goal of your task will define whether you are preparing a proposal, a technical report, or some other type of presentation. Selecting the appropriate document and preparing it in a way that communicates your message and accomplishes your goal are critical to your success.

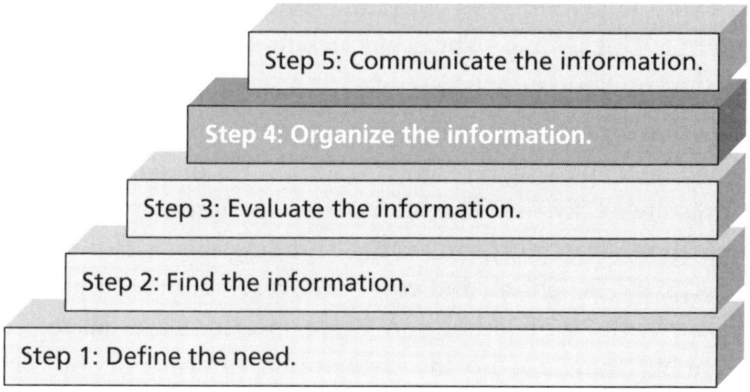

Research Process Step 4: Organize the Information

Once you have determined the appropriate type of document, you must present your information in a logical and coherent manner that holds your audience's attention and brings them to a logical conclusion. The way in which you organize facts and figures, as well as the format in which they are presented, largely determines the response you will receive.

This chapter will introduce you to organizational methods as well as presentations commonly used in professional settings that you may be asked to complete at some time in your career—proposals, technical reports, tables, charts, and multimedia. General concepts of organization will be applied to each and considerations specific to each of the formats will be discussed. Many of the concepts presented here can be applied to other documents and reports that you may encounter.

THE IMPORTANCE OF EFFECTIVE ORGANIZATION OF INFORMATION

Think of a time when you were attempting to understand a piece of information or a document that was poorly organized. Recall the frustration and difficulty you might have felt as you attempted to sort through and use that information. Compare that situation to a time when you used information that was organized methodically and efficiently. Chances are that you experienced less stress, used your time more efficiently, and completed your task more easily and effectively. The manner in which you organize and present information can have the same effect on your audiences.

Information typically is presented to achieve a goal. For example, a researcher who is applying for a grant is seeking funding to complete his or her research activities. The information the researcher presents in the grant application must convince the funding agency that the research is necessary, beneficial, and cost-effective. As another example, a student is asked to write a position paper on a controversial topic. The student will have to provide background information on the issue, compare various positions on the topic, state his or her position with supporting reasoning and explanation, and draw a conclusion. The goal for each project calls for different organizational strategies.

Effectively organized information allows you to be understood, and for the recipient to apply, question, or utilize what you have presented. Information that is organized and presented effectively contributes to productive communication. Productivity on the job also is facilitated by effective organization of information. Reports, proposals, and other documents that clearly communicate relevant facts contribute to efficient completion of tasks and projects. Well-organized information in professional reports and presentations will contribute to the success of your organization as well as your professional development and advancement.

REFLECTION QUESTION

1. Based on your experience, describe an example that demonstrates effective organization of information. Compare that example with an example of ineffective organization of information. What are the differences between the two situations? How did each affect you?

5

ORGANIZATIONAL STRATEGIES

You are more likely to be understood when you organize your information and communication effectively. Material that is organized in a logical and meaningful fashion is more readily used and applied than random, disorganized data (Huitt, 2003). By organizing information systematically, you will maximize the opportunity for your audience to receive an accurate message. For example, a criminal justice student who is describing the events leading up to a crime might choose to organize the information chronologically because this type of organization best conveys the sequence of events leading to the crime. If the same student wants to explore the motives for the crime, however, the information might be organized according to possible cause and effect.

As a presenter of information, you have choices in how information is arranged. Huitt (2003) discusses organization of information as it pertains to learning, and Stucker (2006) approaches organization of information from an applied perspective. Consider the following organizational strategies based on the work of these researchers.

HINT: Consider the goal you wish to achieve by presenting your information. Organize your information in a way that logically leads to your goal.

ORGANIZATION BY CATEGORY OR CONCEPT

Separate ideas that combine to produce a concept must be understood individually before their synthesis makes sense. This calls for **organization by category or concept.** For example, if a student of early childhood education wants to describe a positive classroom environment for kindergarten students, she first might discuss the physical classroom environment, types of activities available to the children, characteristics of the teacher, and a schedule appropriate for this age group. Each element of the positive classroom is discussed in terms of its attributes, why these attributes are important to kindergartners, and techniques for developing each attribute in the classroom. She then pulls together the individual elements and describes a typical day in the kindergarten class. The discussion includes how the separate concepts blend and interact to produce a positive classroom environment. Effectively organized information has provided a clear description of each element and enabled the audience to synthesize them into a coherent concept.

Organization by category or concept also is effective when constructing a case to support a premise. Consider the example of a student in a healthcare management class who is involved in a debate over private versus government-sponsored health insurance coverage. In this example, the student is promoting government-sponsored health programs. He discusses individual themes such as the financial burden of illness and uninsured individuals, the cost-effectiveness of implementing preventive health measures, and strategies for implementing government-sponsored programs. He supports his statements with reliable data that he has researched and evaluated for credibility. The student then brings together his ideas to provide a convincing case for a government-sponsored health program. In this scenario, well-organized information makes the student's case more compelling. Both of these examples use synthesis of ideas to create a concept.

A variation on organization by concept is to begin with a major concept and break it down into the elements that formulate the central idea. Continuing with the example of the early childhood education student, consider that she is presenting information on playground management strategies. In this example, playground management is the major concept. Within that concept, she might talk about setting behavior expectations appropriate to kindergartners, structuring group activities, and addressing safety considerations. This application of organization by concept uses analysis of a concept by breaking it down into its respective parts.

CRITICAL THINKING QUESTIONS

1. What information in your field would be organized most effectively by concept or category? Would you organize this information using synthesis or analysis strategies? Why?
2. Consider a presentation or assignment that you completed recently. How did you implement the concepts? How might you have implemented them further to improve your presentation or assignment?
3. Consider an assignment that you currently are completing or will be starting in the near future. How can you implement organization by category or concept to benefit the assignment?

CHRONOLOGICAL ORGANIZATION

Organization according to time, called **chronological organization,** is used when the sequence of events influences an outcome. A common example is found in the instructions for assembling something such as a model or a piece of furniture. Information provided out of sequence would lead to failure and frustration. And consider the example of a computer technology student who, in a practical exam, is explaining and demonstrating the steps involved in repairing a computer. To be successful, the steps must be explained and executed in a specific sequence. Likewise, the allied health student who is describing or demonstrating a treatment procedure must organize the information in the proper sequence or the treatment is likely to be ineffective.

Often, chronological organization of information is necessary for a sequence of events to make sense and explain an outcome. Consider how effective your next joke would be if you were to give the punch line first and then tell the details of the joke randomly! The example of the criminology student describing the events leading to a crime provides an example of effectively leading to and explaining an outcome using chronological organization.

Certain information that is organized chronologically involves transition from one phase to the next. In these situations, recipients of the information have to understand the progression between steps or stages. For example, a physical therapist assistant student describing the progression of a patient through treatment must organize treatment steps in sequence and also must clarify the relationship of one phase of treatment to the next.

In another example, the student in a human development class is describing the sequence of development in an infant. The developmental stages must be described sequentially, and the information organized and explained to demonstrate the continuity of development. Each of these cases illustrates the importance of information that explains the relationship between the chronological phases.

CRITICAL THINKING QUESTIONS

1. What information in your field would be most effectively organized chronologically? What information in your field would have to be organized with transitional information?
2. Consider a presentation or an assignment that you recently completed. How did you implement these concepts? How might you have implemented them further to improve your presentation or assignment?
3. Consider an assignment that you currently are completing or will be starting in the near future. How can you implement chronological organization to benefit the assignment?

HIERARCHICAL ORGANIZATION

Hierarchical organization is used when information is best conveyed in a specific order, such as from most to least important or least complex to most complex. Bloom's taxonomy, which you first read about in chapter 1, is an example of a hierarchical arrangement beginning with the least complex concepts and progressing to the most complex. Another example is the computer technology student who is describing the process of diagnosing a computer problem. He starts by looking for simple problems, such as a poorly connected cable, and describes progressing to more complex problems, such as examining the processor. A graphics design student uses hierarchical organization when she creates a brochure for a product and lists the various models of the product, beginning with the model having the fewest features and lowest cost and progressing to the model with the most features and highest cost.

CRITICAL THINKING QUESTIONS

1. What information in your field would be most effectively organized hierarchically?
2. Consider a presentation or an assignment that you recently completed. How did you implement these concepts? How might you have implemented them further to improve your presentation or assignment?
3. Consider an assignment that you currently are completing or will be starting in the near future. How can you implement a hierarchical organization to benefit the assignment?

CRITICAL THINKING QUESTIONS

1. What information in your field would be organized most effectively alphabetically?
2. Consider a presentation or assignment that you recently completed. How did you implement these concepts? How might you have implemented them further to improve your presentation or assignment?
3. Consider an assignment that you are currently completing or will be starting in the near future. How can you implement an alphabetical organization to benefit the assignment?

5

ALPHABETICAL ORGANIZATION

Obvious examples of **alphabetical organization** are dictionaries and telephone directories. Alphabetical organization is appropriate when the reader knows the information he or she is looking for and must locate it by a key word. Glossaries and directories are additional examples of situations in which alphabetical organization is effective and appropriate.

In some circumstances you will be presenting pieces of information as equivalent and nonhierarchical in nature. Presenting the information alphabetically represents a method of organization that does not imply any type of order based on any attribute or characteristic. For instance, if you are crediting individuals who contributed to a project, listing them alphabetically avoids the implication that one individual contributed more than another. Or consider the pharmacy technician student who is describing the characteristics of various medications as part of an assignment. By ordering the medications alphabetically, the student avoids any implied hierarchy and makes the list usable because the names of the medications are easily located alphabetically.

Table 5-1 summarizes the strategies discussed for organizing information. Table 5-2 reviews and summarizes Bloom's concepts and suggests how each level of the cognitive domain can be used to guide the information-organization process. Keep these concepts in mind, as the organizational strategies discussed in this section will be described according to Bloom's cognitive domain.

- What am I trying to accomplish by presenting this information? What is my goal?
- What organizational method best supports my goal?
- Is my information best organized according to ideas or concepts that build to a logical conclusion?
- Is my information best organized according to time or in a sequential order?
- Is my information best organized in a hierarchical fashion to show relative importance of the information pieces?
- Is my information best located by a keyword or inappropriate for hierarchical organization?

Organization Method	Description
Organization by Category or Concept	Separate ideas are combined to produce a concept. The synthesis of the individual ideas produces a logical conclusion.
Chronological Organization	Chronological organization is organization according to time. The sequence of events influences or explains an outcome.
Hierarchical Organization	Hierarchical organization is used when information is best conveyed in a specific order. It indicates the relative significance of information, as from most to least important or least complex to most complex.
Alphabetical Organization	Alphabetical organization is appropriate when the reader knows the information he or she is looking for and has to locate it by a key word. It is used to organize information in a manner that does not suggest a hierarchy.

Table 5-1 Summary of Information Organization Strategies

Bloom's Level	Definition	Uses
Knowledge	Provides facts and figures	Presenting factual background information, often as a foundation for more complex ideas
Comprehension	Compares, summarizes, shows an understanding of concepts	Providing examples and explanations of facts and background information
Application	Relates an example or set of rules to an authentic situation	Explaining how something is done; applying a procedure to a set of circumstances
Analysis	Breaks down a concept into its components.	Simplifying a complex concept; showing the components of a complex idea
Synthesis	Creates a new idea or concept from single facts or components	Presenting a new idea; explaining how individual elements combine to create a new concept
Evaluation	Make a judgment about the effectiveness or appropriateness of an idea or concept	Defending or advocating a position or idea; presenting a solution

Table 5-2 Bloom's Taxonomy as a Strategy for Organizing Information

PRESENTING INFORMATION EFFECTIVELY

Information can be presented verbally (orally or written), graphically, or by using multimedia. Your choice of presentation media depends on several factors including your audience, the type of information you are conveying, and the presentation environment.

Be aware that some standards apply to use of all information regardless of the format in which it is presented. For all formats, keep in mind the following considerations, many of which review information from earlier in this chapter as components of organizing information.

- *Organization of the presentation.* The visual organization of your presentation is as important as the way in which the information itself is structured. For example, written documents must be formatted in a manner that maximizes legibility. Graphics and multimedia must be easy to see and clearly understood. Electronic information, such as that presented on web pages, must be intuitively navigated.
- *Ethical and legal considerations.* All information must be referenced properly and sources cited. Information must be used in a way that applies information rather than simply repeats someone else's work. Plagiarism is illegal and unethical in all presentation formats. (Plagiarism and appropriate referencing will be addressed in chapter 6.)
- *Credibility considerations.* Information must come from credible, current, and reliable sources. The evaluation methods discussed in chapters 1 and 4 must be applied to all information used in any presentation.

Selecting your presentation medium carefully will maximize the effectiveness of your information.

- Who is my audience?
- What is the purpose of my presentation?
- What is the presentation environment?
- Does the organization of my presentation maximize its legibility?
- Are my information sources properly cited and referenced?
- Have I ensured that my information comes from current, credible, and reliable sources?

5

ORGANIZING WRITTEN DOCUMENTS

Written presentations include documents such as reports, proposals, needs assessments, and others. As part of effective organization, written work must be presented professionally and in a manner that reflects the standards of your field.

The first step in creating an effective document or presentation is to organize the information in a way in which you can use it. After you have implemented your research strategy, you are likely to have an extensive amount of information. Organizing the material in a way that is useful to you provides the foundation for creating an effective end product. Consider the following suggestions for organizing the information that you have retrieved. You may find that a combination of these strategies will best meet your needs.

HINT: While researching information, implement a method or methods for organizing your data that fits your style and preferences.

- *Know the organization strategy you have selected.* Understanding how you are going to arrange your information will allow you to organize your resources accordingly. For example, if you have decided that chronological organization is most appropriate for your topic, you can sort your resources in an accurate sequence.

5

©Digital Vision

Keeping information organized as you work is critical to presenting information effectively.

If you are organizing information by concept, you may choose to sort your data into folders labeled for each main idea.

- *Use a format that works for you.* Do you find yourself buried in piles of paper on your desk? Do you cringe at the thought of reading documents on the computer screen? Collect your resources in a format that works for you. Some individuals read printed copies more effectively and benefit from making notes on them, highlighting important points. Other people prefer to read documents electronically and take brief notes as they read from the computer screen. Be aware, though, that some information may be available in only one format, so you will have to be flexible. For example, if some of your material is available only in a book and you prefer the electronic documents, you necessarily will have to adapt your preferred method to that format.

- *Use a cataloging system that works for you.* A cataloging system is the system you use to physically organize material. Examples of cataloging systems are note cards, binders, electronic folders, and various types of files. Each has its advantages and shortcomings. For example, individual file folders allow you to easily separate documents into categories that support individual concepts. Your choice will depend on your personal preference and style. Table 5-3 summarizes the advantages and disadvantages of various cataloging systems and gives suggestions for using each.

The manner in which a document is prepared contributes to its organization. Compare a document that uses graphics effectively to a document that uses graphics randomly and haphazardly. Thoughtful and effectively placed graphics add to the clarity and meaning of the document whereas misused graphics can distract and confuse the reader. Consider the following factors when preparing written documents.

- *Follow the recommended style.* Guidelines for writing style come from various sources. Style guides such as *The Chicago Manual of Style, Publication Manual of the American Psychological Association (APA),* and the *Modern Language Association (MLA) Style Manual* provide standards for language use and reference citation. Each profession and field tends to adopt one style consistently. For example, the social science fields generally use the APA style in research papers and journal articles. Preparing and organizing documents in the style used in your field provides readers with a recognized format.

  Style guides also provide consistent formatting elements such as spacing, margins, treatment of graphics, tables, and charts, and other elements. Consistent formatting allows the reader to recognize and locate information more easily.

- *Use language and level of complexity appropriate to your audience.* As much as possible, know who will be reading your finished document or listening to your presentation. For general audiences, use simple language and define terms when necessary. For professional audiences or groups with a more advanced knowledge, use more technical language and terminology. Choosing the level of

CRITICAL THINKING QUESTIONS

Imagine that you are preparing to give two presentations. One will be for new graduates just getting started in your field, and the other will be for seasoned professionals.

1. What differences would you make in the two presentations?
2. How could you use Bloom's taxonomy to organize the information in each of the presentations?

Cataloging System	Advantages	Disadvantages	Suggested Uses
Note cards	• Convenient for recording one idea or fact per card. • Small size allows opportunity to sort and rearrange information.	• Numerous cards can be difficult to manage.	• Arrange events chronologically • Arrange information hierarchically • Arrange information alphabetically. • Elaborate on a single idea or concept per card to effectively organize information.
Binders	• Documents can be stored and reviewed in original form • All information is kept in one place. • Addition of divider tabs allows efficient organization of information.	• Sorting information by individual facts is more difficult in full document form.	• Create a section of information for each concept or idea.
Electronic folders	• Use of paper is minimized • Information can be retrieved and reorganized with relative ease	• May not be readily accessible without computer. If documents are bookmarked, will require Internet access.	• Sort information by concept or idea. • Rearrange and duplicate information to meet a different need.
Individual file folders	• Documents can be stored and reviewed in original form • Information can be easily rearranged as needed and to serve various purposes	• Can be challenging to keep multiple individual folders together.	• Create a folder for each idea or concept. • Create a separate folder for a designated time period, and organize information chronologically.
Expandable files	• Documents can be stored and reviewed in original form • Information can be kept in one place.	• Can be bulky.	• Use in ways similar to individual files.
Visual organizers	• Effective for visual and kinesthetic learners • Information can be easily rearranged. • Provides a view of the "big picture."	• Not easily transported. • May be less effective for verbal learners. • Difficult to include in-depth detail.	• Show relationships between concepts • Create as a timeline.

Table 5-3 Information Cataloging Systems

Some of the more commonly used techniques for cataloging information are summarized here, and you may be aware of others.

language appropriate to your audience is closely related to selecting an appropriate level of resources for the type of project you are completing (see chapter 5). For general audiences, you are more likely to use language and organizational strategies based on the less complex levels of Bloom's taxonomy; for example, and with more seasoned professionals, the organization based on more advanced levels of the taxonomy is appropriate.

You probably will agree that the presentation for new graduates should be more basic than the presentation for seasoned professionals. New members of a profession tend to need straightforward facts and information as they learn about the field. Facts, examples, and other information that provides a foundation for learning are appropriate for individuals who are learning about a field. Based on Bloom's taxonomy, you would organize your information according to the lower levels of the cognitive domain and use the knowledge, comprehension, and possible application levels.

More advanced members of the profession can be expected to have the foundational knowledge and to be using it to assess situations, solve problems creatively, and evaluate circumstances. For these professionals, you likely would organize information based on the higher levels of Bloom's taxonomy, such as analysis, synthesis, and evaluation. As might be expected, more experienced professionals are able to use information in a more complex manner. Thus, you can use Bloom's taxonomy to organize information differently, in a way that meets the needs of your audience.

Language use also must be considered in terms of your audience. If you use highly technical language, you probably will lose an audience of people who are inexperienced in your field. Consider the example of a physician explaining a complex medical issue to a patient. Unless the patient is a medical professional with the appropriate background, the physician will have to use language that the patient can understand if he or she is to understand and comply with treatment. Conversely, language that is too simple may not hold the interest of a more knowledgeable audience and may be insulting to their level of expertise.

- *Organize information from simple to complex.* Organizing information from simple to complex provides a foundation on which the recipient of the information can build more complex concepts. Suppose you are teaching someone to drive. Before starting the ignition, you will provide basic information about the car, including where the various controls are located and activated, how to adjust the mirrors and seat, and basics about steering, turning, and other factors in controlling the car. Next, you might ask the learner to review the information you have provided and repeat what you have described to indicate understanding. All of this is done before asking the new driver to actually drive the car.

After the learner has actually driven the car, you might ask him or her to compare the actual driving experience to what he or she thought it would be like and to consider how this insight will contribute to the learning experience. As the learner practices and further develops driving skills, you will ask him or her to solve problems commonly encountered on the road and to assess his or her progress. By organizing the information from simple to complex, you have led the learner from the basics of driving to being able to problem-solve and evaluate various driving situations. Table 5-4 illustrates how this example reflects Bloom's taxonomy.

- *Follow conventional language, spelling, and grammar standards.* Professionals should avoid slang and unorthodox spelling and grammar. The use of recognized language standards contributes to the perception of well-organized information. Imagine that you were reading a document containing slang from the 1950s and 1960s. Although you might be entertained and amused, how seriously would you take the information? Of course, using an occasional slang word for emphasis can be an effective tool. Generally, however, language should follow standard guidelines. Guidelines for language conventions, as we said, can be found in the style guide (APA, MLA, etc.) used in your field. Finally, you should respect elements of diversity and incorporate them appropriately in the context of your document or presentation.
- *Check for accuracy.* In organizing information, you must ensure its accuracy to maximize the usefulness of the information and minimize the chances of misquoting sources. Information that is clear and correct contributes to a well-received document or presentation and affects your credibility as an information provider.
- *Use graphics that are clear and enhance the content of the document.* Thoughtfully selected graphics can enhance the clarity of

Level in Bloom's Taxonomy	Step of Teaching Driving a Car	Explanation
Knowledge	The learner receives basic information about the car, such as where the controls are located, how to adjust the mirrors and seat, and basics about steering, turning, and other factors in controlling the car	The new driver learns the facts that are foundational to maneuvering the car effectively and safely.
Comprehension	The learner reviews or summarizes the information provided and gives some examples.	The new driver translates the basic knowledge into his or her own words and, in doing so, explains and demonstrates an understanding of the concepts.
Application	The learner actually drives the car.	The new driver puts the newly learned concepts to use.
Analysis	The learner compares the actual driving experience to what he or she thought it would be like.	The new driver compares and contrasts the experience with his or her expectations, and assesses each element of the driving experience.
Synthesis	The learner considers how this insight will contribute to the learning experience. The learner solves problems commonly encountered on the road.	The new driver integrates what they have learned with their own ideas and develops new concepts about the driving experience. The learner combines concepts to formulate solutions to problems.
Evaluation	The learner assesses his or her progress.	The new driver compares his or her proficiency to acceptable standards of skill and safety and makes an assessment of the skills he or she needs to develop.

Table 5-4 Simple-to-Complex Organization Related to Bloom's Taxonomy

information, in contrast to randomly placed graphics, which detract from your message. When considering the use of graphics in the overall organization of your document or presentation, we first must consider how the graphics mesh with the written text.

HINT: Use Bloom's Taxonomy to determine the appropriate level of complexity of information for your audience. Generally, audiences with less experience will benefit from information structured at the lower levels of the taxonomy, while more experienced audiences are likely to benefit from information organized at the higher levels.

Graphics should be clearly related to the information in the text, convey an accurate message, and effectively communicate without having to read the text.

ORGANIZING GRAPHICS

Graphics—figures, tables, charts—must be appropriate to the content of your document or presentation and accurately convey the message you are sending. After you have determined where a graphic is appropriate in your overall organizational plan, you must effectively organize the information represented in the graphic. Any documentation or sources for the data should be included in full. Graphics that contribute to the clarity of your document or presentation have the following characteristics, based on the work of Klass (2002).

- *The reader can easily understand the graphic.* The graphic must clearly communicate a message. If the graphic is comparing or explaining data, the type of data must be stated clearly and the relationships among the data illustrated clearly.
- *The graphic elaborates on the information in the document or presentation.* There must be a clear relationship between the graphic and the information that you are conveying. For example, if you are comparing two sets of data, a good choice might be a graph to clearly illustrate the differences between the two sets.
- *The image is selected for its ability to convey an accurate message.* Your choice of a graphic will depend on the type of information

you want to convey. For example, a pie chart, which illustrates the relationship of parts to the whole, could be the best way to show the percentages of religious groups represented in the United States. (Examples of commonly used charts, tables, and other graphics and their uses will be outlined in "Types of Graphics.")

- *A table, chart, or graphic is able to stand alone.* A reader should be able to understand the information presented in a table or chart without referring to the text of the document for additional explanation. The meaning of data represented must be clearly defined. The table or chart should allow the reader to form conclusions from the data.
- *A table or chart simplifies information.* A value of tables, charts, and figures is in simplifying information that would be confusing if it were explained only in the text. As an example, refer to Table 5-4 in this chapter. Review the information it contains and imagine how long and convoluted the information could be if presented in sentence format. To determine whether the information is best expressed in a table or chart, write out the information in sentences. If this is confusing to read, or if you become frustrated in writing it, chances are that it would be best represented in a table or a graphic. If the information can be expressed effectively in text, a graphic may be unnecessary.
- *An effective graphic should be as simple as possible.* Use the simplest form that conveys the data accurately. Avoid extraneous colors, lines, and other embellishments that can detract from the meaningfulness of the data.
- *Data are presented in relationship to a context.* Context adds to the meaning of data by showing how the data relate to a standard, category, or other framework. A graphic should provide information that explains the context to which the data relate.
- *Pictures or cartoons illustrate ideas in the text.* Some information has more impact when it is conveyed in an image. Political cartoons provide an example. The political cartoons on the editorial page of the newspaper generally would not be as entertaining if their message were described in the text. Like tables, charts, and other graphics, images (pictures and cartoons) are used most effectively when they simplify a concept or emphasize a point that has been discussed in the text.

success steps

ORGANIZING GRAPHICS EFFECTIVELY

Organize graphics so

- the reader can easily understand the graphic.
- the graphic elaborates on the information in the document or presentation.
- the image is selected for its ability to convey an accurate message.
- a table or chart or figure is able to stand alone.
- a table or chart or figure simplifies information.
- the graphic is as simple as possible.
- data are presented in relationship to a context.
- pictures or cartoons illustrate ideas in the text.

TYPES OF GRAPHICS

Of the many types of graphics that can be used in documents and presentations, each has its advantages for conveying various kinds of information. Consider the following examples of graphics that are available.

- **Bar charts** (also called column charts or histograms) are used for comparing data by varying the length of the columns or bars. Bar charts can be drawn vertically or horizontally. Figure 5-1 provides an example of a bar chart. Variations of bar charts include simple column charts, stacked column charts, and 100% stacked bar charts. Electronic programs such as Microsoft Excel allow users to apply 3-D effects, color, labels, and legends to bar charts.
- **Line charts** typically display a trend over time. Typically, time is represented on the X axis of the graph and the element being measured over time is represented on the Y axis. Figure 5-2 is an example of a line chart. In addition to simple line charts, variations on line charts include stacked line charts and 100% stacked line charts. As was the case with bar charts, computer programs such as Microsoft Excel allow the user to apply 3-D effects, along with markers at each data point, color, and legends.
- **Pie charts** show the contribution of each value to a total, allowing the reader to understand the relationship of parts to the

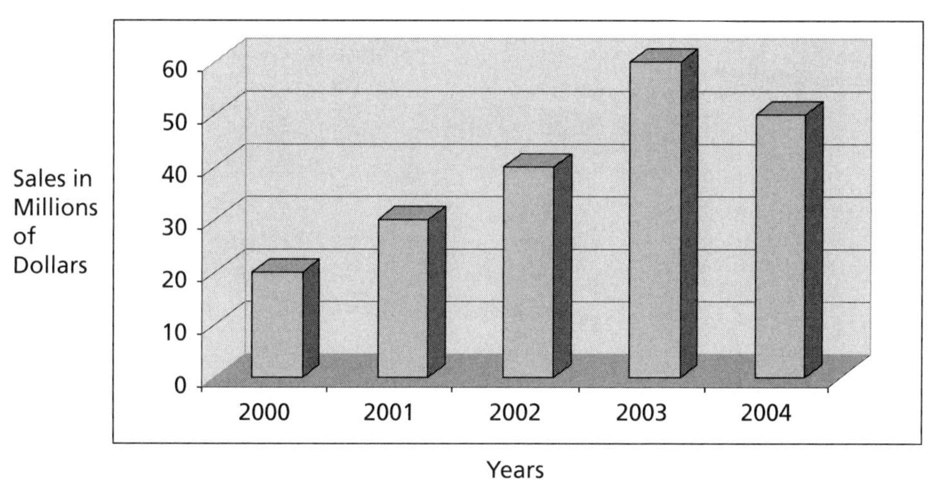

Figure 5-1 Example of a Bar Chart

This bar chart shows the sales of a company over the course of five years. By comparing the length of the bars, the reader can easily compare the sales between years.

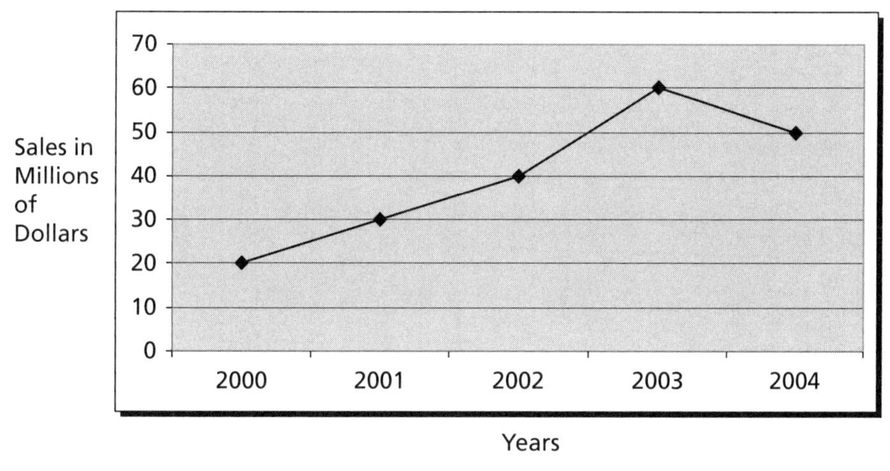

Figure 5-2 Example of a Line Chart

This line chart shows the same sales of a company represented in Figure 5-1. Instead of comparing the length of the bars, the reader can easily track the sales over time. The line connecting the data points clearly indicates the trend over time.

whole. An example of a pie chart is provided in Figure 5-3. Types of pie charts include the simple pie chart, an exploded pie chart, and a bar of a pie chart. As with other types of charts, you can add 3-D effects, color, labels, and legends, as desired.

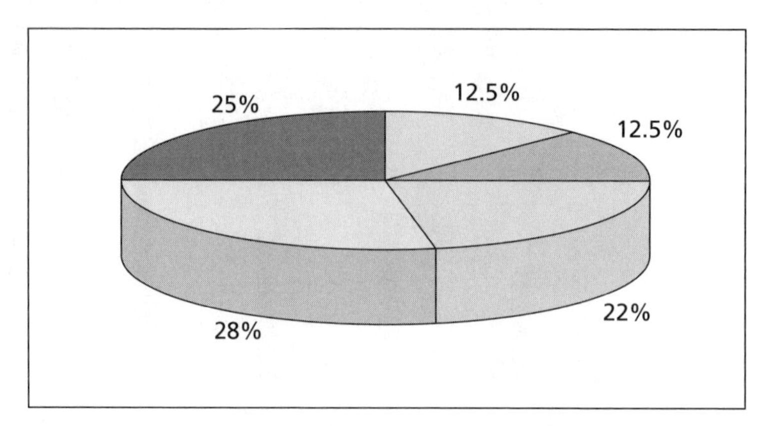

Figure 5-3 Example of a Pie Chart

Each section of this pie chart shows the percentage of various elements that make up the whole. Note that the visual size of each slice accurately represents the numbered percentages noted on the chart. This representation portrays a three-dimensional pie chart, but the same information could be represented in a simple two-dimensional chart.

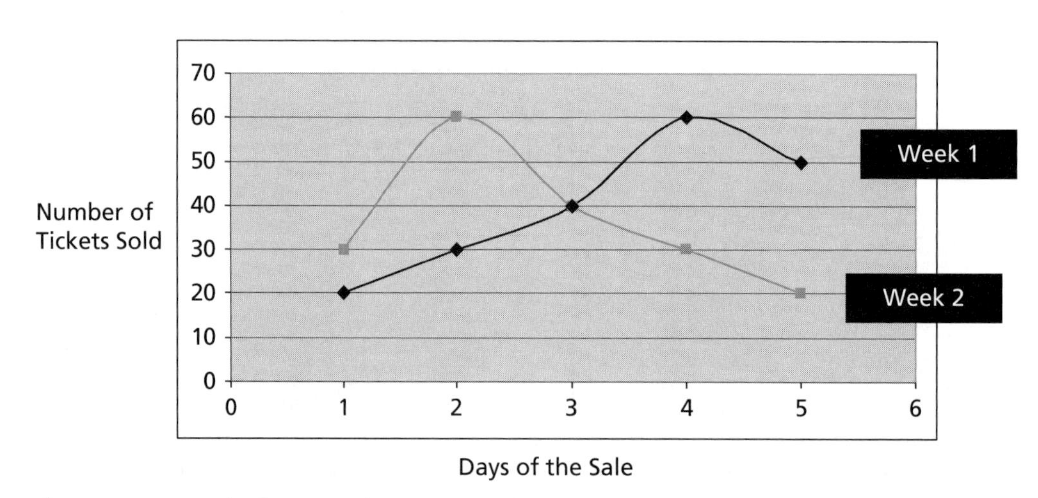

Figure 5-4 Example of a Scatter Chart

This scatter chart compares the number of tickets sold on each day of a two-week period. The lines have been added using Microsoft Excel.

- **Scatter charts** (sometimes called scatter plots) compare pairs of values under the same situations. A scatter chart is illustrated in Figure 5-4.
- **Area charts** display trends and their magnitude over time, as illustrated in Figure 5-5. Area charts are similar to line charts, except that the area below the line is filled in. You can add 3-D

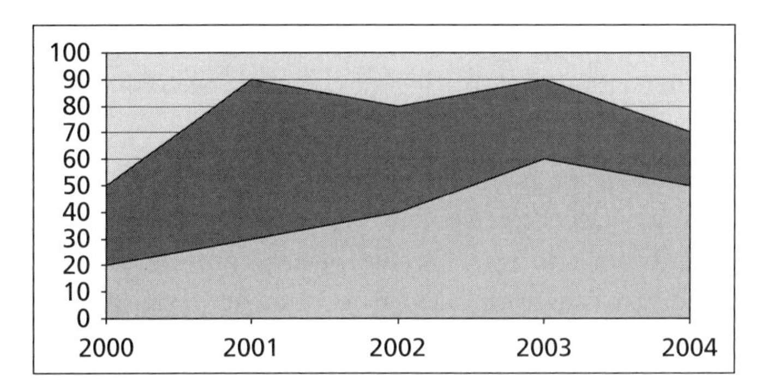

Figure 5-5 Example of an Area Chart

On this area chart, each filled area represents a value over time. The peak of each filled area represents the value (on the Y axis) of the categories represented on the X axis.

effects, color, legends, labels, and animation to this type of chart, using Microsoft Excel.

> **HINT:** When using a graphic to present information, select the simplest graphic that effectively communicates your message.

ORGANIZING POWERPOINT PRESENTATIONS

Presentation software such as Microsoft PowerPoint provides opportunities to create impressive and fairly sophisticated presentations. When using presentation software, two levels of organization must be considered. First, content must be organized in a logical and understandable manner, using the concepts discussed in this chapter. In addition, visual and spatial organization is important when using presentation software. The visual appeal of an electronic presentation has a significant impact on audience members and their response to the presentation.

The suggestions presented here are only general guidelines, and straying from the rules can increase the impact of your presentation at times. For example, black, orange, and lime green are not typically recommended as a good color combination for a entire PowerPoint presentation, but if you use these colors on one slide that refers to the pop culture of the 1960s, they can emphasize your message. Good judgment in considering your topic, audience, and other factors is always essential to creating effective presentations. Consider the following recommendations for creating an effective PowerPoint presentation (Montecino, 1999).

- *Select colors thoughtfully.* Color choice can have a significant effect on how viewers receive your presentation. For example, text that is difficult to read because of low contrast with the background may cause your viewers to "tune out" your presentation because it is too difficult to follow. Keep in mind the following points about color in your presentations.
  - Select color combinations that provide enough contrast to facilitate reading but are not so high contrast that they become distracting. Select colors that promote legibility.
  - Avoid colors that clash or form an unusual combination. Unorthodox color combinations can be effective if used sparingly and to support a specific theme but should not be used consistently or for an entire presentation.

  Review Figure 5-6 for various examples of effective color choices.
- *Use legible fonts.* The text in a presentation must be legible to all members of audience, yet not so large as to be overwhelming.

Slide 1: Low-contrast colors are difficult to read.

Figure 5-6 Examples of Use of Color in PowerPoint

Effective PowerPoint slides should use basic colors with enough contrast for viewers to see the slide elements clearly. These examples show how color can be used on slides to advantage or disadvantage.

Slide 2: This color combination is unconventional and difficult to read.

Slide 3: The conventional colors of blue and white are pleasing to the eye and are easily read.

Figure 5-6 (*Continued*)

To maximize legibility, consider font size and style. Figure 5-7 provides examples.

- The recommended font size in a presentation is 22–48 points. Smaller font sizes become difficult to read, and larger font sizes may become overwhelming and be difficult to fit on the slide.

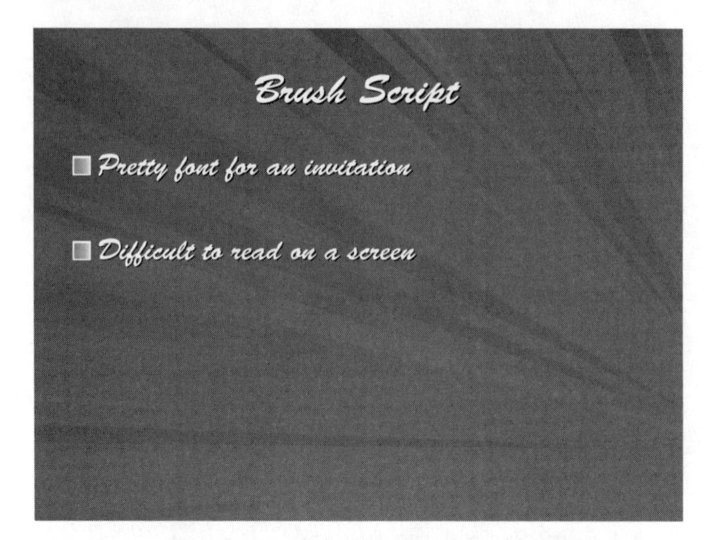

Slide 1 shows an embellished font that is difficult to read on the screen.

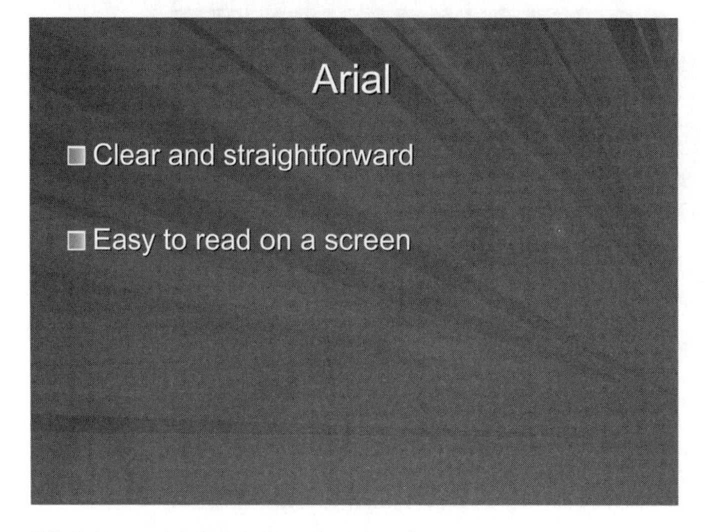

Slide 2 shows a plain font that is easily read on the screen.

Figure 5-7 Examples of Fonts in PowerPoint
Compare Slide 1 with Slide 2, which are different fonts of the same size

- Fonts should be of a standard and plain style, such as Arial or Times Roman. Intricate and embellished fonts are difficult to read on a screen.

- *Present information clearly and concisely.* Slides are only one part of the overall presentation. In addition, you will be explaining and possibly demonstrating the main points represented on the slides. Therefore, you should consider the slides as a supplement to guide viewers through the information you are presenting. To use the slides effectively, consider the following recommendations.

- Set a limit of six lines per slide and six words per line. Capture the main idea and state it succinctly. Expand on each idea orally.
- Use phrases versus sentences. Again, these are main ideas to guide the viewer. Your explanation will provide the details.
- State main ideas using larger font. PowerPoint automatically adjusts the font size as the levels of text decrease. In keeping with that aid, state the main idea on the higher levels of the PowerPoint outline and supporting ideas underneath. The main idea will be in larger font and the supporting ideas in smaller font.
- Limit punctuation, and avoid abbreviations that might be unclear to viewers.
- Do not use all capitals or all lower case letters. DO use conventional grammar rules.

Create visual appeal. The general organization and appearance of your presentation have an impact on your audience. The following are suggestions for creating an effective and professional presentation.

- Select a plain or simple background that does not compete with your message. A solid color or a watermark background that supports your theme is appropriate. Bold and busy backgrounds make the text hard to read and distract the audience from your message.
- Avoid distracting slide transitions, text appearances, and sounds. If you do choose to use one of the custom features available in PowerPoint, select one that is subtle and that is consistent with the tone and message of your presentation.
- Be consistent. If you do choose to use a custom feature, use it throughout the presentation.
- As with written documents, use graphics only if they support the text and the theme of the presentation. Limit graphics to one or two per slide.

CRITICAL THINKING QUESTIONS

1. What is the best PowerPoint presentation you have seen? What made it effective?
2. What is the worst PowerPoint presentation you have seen? What made it ineffective?

HINT: Watch your PowerPoint presentation yourself before presenting to an audience. Evaluate it for legibility, clarity, and visual appeal. View the presentation from various perspectives to ensure that it is clearly visible from all vantage points.

ORGANIZING WEB PAGES

To hold interest, web pages rely extensively on visual organization for navigability. Consider your own experiences using the web. If a page is difficult to interpret and navigate, how long will you stay with it before you are off in search of another page? Organization plays a significant role in the success—and often the profitability—of web pages. The following considerations for effective web page organization are based on Lynch and Horton (2002a, 2002b, 2002c).

5

- *Seek a balance.* Because web pages are a visual medium, visual appeal is a primary consideration. At the same time, information must be meaningful to viewers, capture their attention, and compel further exploration of the site. An effective website offers an appropriate blend of intriguing graphics, informative text, and interactive elements that can be used intuitively.
- *Create a visual hierarchy.* Understanding how viewers see a web page is important in understanding how a web page should be organized to maximize visual appeal.
  - When viewing a web page, readers move from the general to the specific and from the top of the page to the bottom. Readers see color and larger shapes first.
  - Specific information is first noted in graphics.
  - Last, readers refer to text for additional information.
- *Organize visual elements according to the visual hierarchy.* An understanding of the visual hierarchy provides guidance for applying general principles to page design and organization.
  - Use contrasting colors. A subtle background color is recommended (Lynch & Horton, 2002c). Keep in mind that because the reader sees blocks of color first, the reader's eye is drawn to specific information. Therefore, use bolder colors to emphasize specific elements on the page.

- Place your most intriguing graphics at the top of the page. Follow the guideline that any graphic you use should be relevant to the material in the website.
- Use embellishments sparingly. Overuse of embellishments tends to clutter the page and can diminish the emphasis placed on important elements. If everything is embellished, nothing stands out.

- *Include fixed elements.* Fixed elements are pieces of information that are standard to websites and essential to credibility. Fixed elements include the author's name, professional affiliation, contact information, and publication and revision dates of the information.

REFLECTION QUESTIONS

1. What catches your eye when you visit a website?
2. What do you find distracting on a website?
3. What sends you away from a website? How long do you typically stay on a website that is difficult to navigate or understand?

5

APPLICATION AND USES OF ORGANIZED INFORMATION

Organized information has several standard uses in the professional world. Proposals, grants, and technical reports are standard documents common to many fields. Each has a standard format and uses information in specific ways. Understanding how each form uses

Using a standard format for thoughtful preparation of grants, proposals, and technical reports maximizes the effectiveness of your presentation.

various types of information will maximize your effectiveness in preparing or reviewing these documents. You may encounter other types and applications of information in the workplace. Proposals, grants, and technical reports are covered here.

PROPOSALS AND GRANTS

Proposals typically are written to suggest a program or action. Grants are written to obtain funding for research or project. Proposals and grants will be covered together here, as their organization and the information they contain are similar. Specific elements of a grant or proposal will vary depending on the situation. General components and the information contained in each are presented here. The components used as an example here are based on guidelines from the *Catalog of Federal Domestic Assistance* (n.d.)

- *Summary:* Typically, the Summary of a proposal is brief (several paragraphs) and provides an overview of the proposed project. Because the summary is the first page of the proposal, it makes the first impression. Therefore, effective organization of information and presentation of the primary objectives of the project are critical.
- *Introduction:* The Introduction of a proposal is its foundation and plays a significant role in establishing your credibility. The introduction provides general information about participants in the project, the organization, organizational goals, and a history of the organization's activities. Use Bloom's *knowledge* level of the cognitive domain to organize the introduction.
- *Statement of Problem and Purpose:* This section of a proposal clearly describes the problem or issue that is being addressed, as well as the benefits that the program will provide. Other issues that typically are addressed in this section include a brief history of the problem, current programs that address it, and how the current proposal supplements these programs. It is also important to present alternatives for continuing the program when current funding is depleted. Bloom's stage of *analysis* and critical thinking skills are used in this phase.
- *Objectives:* The Objectives section states what the project is intended to achieve and the methods that will be used to meet the

goals. Goals must be measurable and realistic, and the project will be evaluated based on how effectively the stated goals are met. Creating feasible and meaningful goals requires the synthesis of needs, reality, and creative thinking and ideas.

- *Action Plan:* This section of the proposal relies heavily on Bloom's level of *synthesis*. The Action Plan outlines the sequence of activities that will lead to achievement of the goals. Graphics such as a flowchart or table can be used to effectively explain the sequence of project events.
- *Evaluation:* The Evaluation phase of a project covers evaluation of the final product as well as the process leading to it. Projects typically are evaluated on how well they met the objectives and goals, how closely the plans were followed, and how the project met the needs stated at the beginning of the project. Bloom's *evaluation* stage from the cognitive domain is a way to think about organizing information for this last stage of a proposal.

TECHNICAL REPORTS

Technical reports are common in the workplace to communicate the results of a project or research. Technical reports typically contain the following elements and are organized accordingly (Sherman, 1996), with some variation depending on your situation.

- *Title:* The title should be concise, yet describe the content of the report.
- *Author information:* The author's name, title, professional affiliation, and contact information should be provided.
- *Abstract:* The abstract is a brief, yet thorough overview of the report's contents. The abstract summarizes the findings and results and can be used as a concise version of the entire paper. Writing an effective abstract requires strong analysis and synthesis skills.
- *Keywords:* The keywords provide parameters of the report and may be used to search for additional information on the topic.
- *Body of the report:* The body of the report contains all the relevant information. Depending on the type of information, the written body of the report can be organized in a variety of ways, as described in this chapter. For example, a research project might be

organized chronologically. The body of the report requires skills related to Bloom's levels of *application, analysis,* and *synthesis* as you explain what you did, your findings, your interpretations, and explanation of new ideas that emerge from your work.

- *Acknowledgements:* In this section, you recognize and express appreciation to individuals who helped or supported you in your project.
- *References:* Documentation of sources referred to are completed according to the guidelines of the recommended style book.
- *Appendices:* Documents that support your report, but that did not flow with the body of the report, are included as appendices. Appendices should be referenced in the text according to your style book.

5

In the scenario at the beginning of this chapter, Anna Hensley had to organize and present information on a series of trends in her company. Initially, she was concerned about how to organize and present the information. After considering the type of information she would be presenting and the goal of her presentation, Anna decided to organize the information by concept and synthesize it into recommendations for company growth. She presented her information in a professional PowerPoint presentation accompanied by handouts and an oral narrative of the slide content.

HINT: If you are required to develop a specialized report, follow the guidelines provided to you. Additional information may be found online by conducting a search using the type of report you are doing as your search term.

learning activities

Activity #1: Creating a Visual Organizer

***Goal:** To create and use a visual organizer to organize information.*

STEP 1: Select a topic for which you would like to organize information. The topic should be fairly complex, and you should have a genuine need to organize the information related to the topic.

STEP 2: Research visual organizers on the Internet. Suggested search terms are "visual organizers" and "concept maps."

STEP 3: Select a visual organizer that suits your needs and learning style. Use it to organize the information related to your topic. You may want to use several organizers to see which is most helpful to you.

Activity #2: Selecting the Best Way To Present Data

Goal: To select the most effective presentation methods for various types of information.

STEP 1. Distribute three small index cards to each group member. Ask each group member to record one type of data on each of the cards. The data should be representative of an aspect of your field.

STEP 2. Randomly select from the completed cards. As a group, decide which graphic would best convey the information. Support your choice with a rationale.

STEP 3. Create the graphic you decide on. Make sure that it meets the criteria for an effective graphic. Decide on the type of graphic, color choice, added effects, labels and legends, and so forth. Explain how your choices enhance the presentation of the information.

STEP 4. Complete as many versions of steps 2 and 3 as possible.

Activity #3: Creating a PowerPoint Presentation

Goal: To apply suggested practices for creating an effective PowerPoint presentation.

STEP 1: Select a topic that is of interest to you and that you would like to present in a PowerPoint presentation.

(continued)

5

STEP 2. Create a PowerPoint presentation on your topic according to the guidelines recommended in this chapter. Seek additional information if needed.

STEP 3. Present your PowerPoint to an audience. Ask viewers to give a constructive critique of your work.

Activity #4: Web Page Exploration

Goal: To develop an awareness of effective web page design and organization

STEP 1. Review as many web pages as possible related to a topic of interest.

STEP 2. Evaluate each website according to the criteria listed in the chapter. Print the page and record your observations directly on the page.

STEP 3. Review your observations and determine which sites were appealing and why. Compile a reference of web page design tips and ideas that you can use in the future.

LEARNING OBJECTIVES REVISITED

Review the learning objectives for this chapter, and rate your level of achievement for each objective using the rating scale provided below. For each objective on which you do not rate yourself as a 3, outline a plan of action that you will take to fully achieve the objective. Include a timeframe for this plan.

1 = did not successfully achieve objective

2 = understand what is needed, but need more study or practice

3 = achieved learning objective thoroughly

	1	2	3
Explain the purpose and importance of effective information organization.	☐	☐	☐
Describe methods of organizing verbal and visual information.	☐	☐	☐
Select and apply an appropriate method for organizing information.	☐	☐	☐
Describe uses of information and the considerations that should be made when organizing information for each use. information skills in school and in the workplace.	☐	☐	☐

Steps to Achieve Unmet Objectives

Steps	Due Date
1. ______________________________	__________
2. ______________________________	__________
3. ______________________________	__________
4. ______________________________	__________

POTENTIAL ITEMS FOR LEARNING PORTFOLIO

Refer to the "Developing Portfolios" section at the front of this text for more information on learning portfolios. Consider adding the following results from this chapter's learning activities or even ideas of your own to your learning portfolio.

REFERENCES

Catalog of Federal Domestic Assistance (n.d.). Developing and writing a grant proposal. Retrieved February 26, 2007 from http://12.46.245.173/pls/portal30/CATALOG.GRANT_PROPOSAL_DYN.show

Huitt, W. (2003). The information processing approach to cognition. *Educational Psychology Interactive*. Valdosta, GA: Valdosta State University. Retrieved May 31, 2006 from http://chiron.valdosta.edu/whuitt/col/cogsys/infoproc.html

Klass, G. (2002). Presenting data: Tabular and graphic display of social indicators—constructing good tables. Retrieved May 30, 2006 from http://lilt.ilstu.edu/gmklass/pos138/datadisplay/sections/goodtables.htm

Lynch, P., & Horton, S. (2002a). Page design. *Web Style Guide,* 2nd ed. Retrieved June 7, 2006 from http://webstyleguide.com/page/index.html

Lynch, P., & Horton, S. (2002b). Visual hierarchy. *Web Style Guide,* 2nd ed. Retrieved June 7, 2006 from http://webstyleguide.com/page/hierarchy.html

Lynch, P. & Horton, S. (2002c). General design considerations. *Web Style Guide,* 2nd ed. Retrieved June 7, 2006 from http://webstyleguide.com/page/general.html

Montecino, V. (1999). Creating an effective PowerPoint presentation. Retrieved June 6, 2006 from http://mason.gmu.edu/~montecin/powerpoint.html

Sherman, A. (1996). Some advice on writing a technical report. Retrieved May 30, 2006 from http://www.cs.umbc.edu/~sherman/Courses/documents/TR_how_to.html

Stucker, C. (2006). Organizing information the way people use it. EzineArticles.com. Retrieved May 31, 2006 from http://ezinearticles.com/?Organizing-Information-the-Way-People-Use-It&id=113311

5

CHAPTER OUTLINE

6

Legal, Ethical, and Communication Issues Related to Information

THE BIG PICTURE

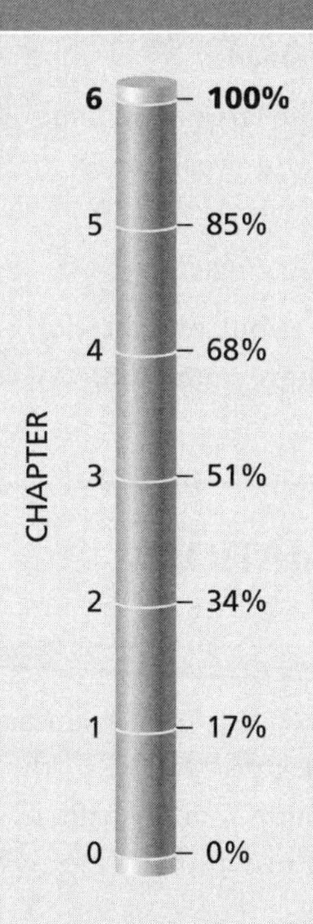

LEARNING OBJECTIVES

By the end of this chapter, students will achieve the following objectives:

- Explain how privacy and security can be breached and protected in both print and electronic environments.
- Explain intellectual property, copyright, and fair use of copyrighted material and how they relate to using information legally and ethically.
- Explain ways to participate appropriately in electronic discussions and live presentations.

©Digital Vision

Professionals frequently are asked to present information to individuals or groups.

6

CHAPTER 6 SCENARIO

Ian Smith was asked to conduct research and present a report of his findings to the management team of the commercial construction company where he is employed. The question he was asked to research involved the market and building projections and obstacles in a specific geographic area of the state. He was instructed to back up his findings with hard, current, and verifiable data and to present the material in a manner that would both inform the management team of the current statistics and persuade them to consider the area for additional commercial building projects. Ian was asked to deliver this information to the small management team, and also to be prepared to present the information at a larger building professional conference in the near future.

Imagine yourself in Ian's place. Answer the following questions thoughtfully and honestly:

- How well will you be able to document that you have provided credible and current resources?
- How well do you think you will perform in a small group meeting of managers when asked to present your information? How will you come across? What are your speaking and presentation strengths and weaknesses in this environment?
- How well do you think you will do in the large conference presentation? Where are your strengths and weaknesses in this environment?
- How do you come across to other professionals?
- How well do you think you can present your presentation in a written format so the managers will have something to take from the meeting to study?

COMMUNICATING INFORMATION LEGALLY AND ETHICALLY

As we have discussed so far, an information-literate individual knows how to define the need for research, find the information in the library or on the Internet, evaluate the information, and organize the information. The last critical component of information literacy is the ability to use information legally and ethically and communicate it effectively to others—Step 5 in the research process. Legal and ethical aspects of information include the concepts of intellectual property, copyright, and fair use. Additional legal and ethical considerations involve privacy and security issues when communicating information.

Effective transmission of information also means that the information is communicated so the receiver can understand the information. A solid understanding of the basic communication process applied specifically to presenting information ensures that the appropriate channels are used in the most effective ways. This chapter addresses these aspects of communicating the information found during the research process. It is not meant to provide legal counsel or advice but is intended only to discuss the types of issues that you, as an information-literate professional, should consider.

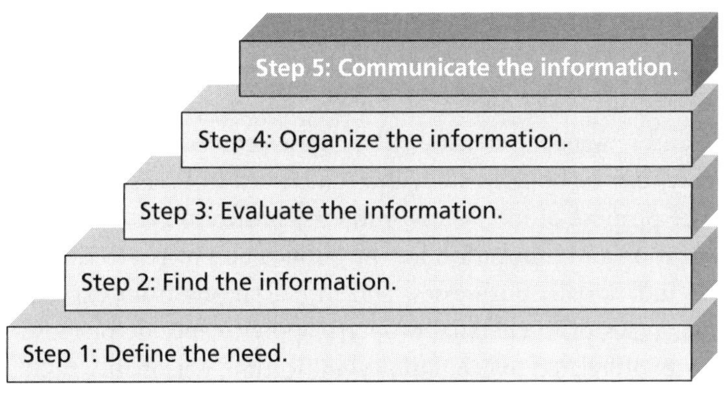

Research Process Step 5: Communicate the Information
The last step of a research project should be to effectively organize the information.

INTELLECTUAL PROPERTY

Intellectual property refers to anything created by the mind, such as literary works (books, poems, essays), artwork (drawings, paintings), inventions, ideas, logos or symbols, names, designs, and images or photographs. In general, the concept of intellectual property treats anything created by the mind (or intellect) the same as any material property and gives rights to owners of intellectual property similar to the rights of owners of material property. When conducting research and using information, then, you have to respect the intellectual property of others, or things others have thought of. Likewise, if you create something, your own creation becomes your intellectual property that others must respect.

The two major areas of intellectual property are **industrial property** and **copyright.** Industrial property refers to intellectual property created in the line of conducting business or for business purposes, such as inventions, trademarks, and industrial and business designs. An **invention** is any idea or concept that is new, useful, and not obvious. A **patent** is a legal protection of the invention and gives the inventor exclusive rights to develop and sell the invention commercially to make a profit for a designated period of time. An inventor must apply for and receive a patent. A **trademark** is a legal protection by which businesses distinguish their products and services from one another, through logos, names, symbols, or other identifying elements, and retain the rights to use the element exclusively in the course of their business. **Industrial design rights** protect the aesthetics or appearance, design, or style of the originator.

Copyright protects other forms of intellectual property, such as literary works, artwork, music, audio and video productions, photographs, and newspaper articles. All of these protections of intellectual property can be bought, sold, and transferred or licensed to third parties. The purpose of intellectual-property protection laws is to encourage creation and innovation for the public good by protecting the producing individuals, businesses, and organizations from exploitation. Other types of intellectual property apply to specific purposes, such as materials related to geographical indication, personality rights, plant breeders' rights, trade secrets, and others. Most relevant to the discussion in this chapter is copyright and its implications in the use and communication of information.

REFLECTION QUESTIONS

1. What intellectual property have you created yourself that you would not like others to use without your permission?
2. How would you feel if someone else were to present your intellectual creations as their own? Write down your feelings.

COPYRIGHT

Copyright reflects the rights given to creators of some forms of expressions of intellectual property, such as literary and artistic works. Copyrights are protected by copyright laws. Ideas are not copyrighted; only the expression of those ideas in some documented format can be copyrighted. Ideas in the form of procedures, methods, facts, techniques, styles, and mathematical concepts cannot be copyrighted. Figure 6-1 gives examples of expressions covered by copyright law.

The goal of a copyright is to protect the original creators of the work (and their heirs). Copyright law is founded in the Intellectual

▪ novels	▪ films
▪ poems	▪ paintings
▪ plays	▪ drawings
▪ reference works	▪ photographs
▪ articles in periodicals	▪ sculptures
▪ computer programs	▪ architecture
▪ databases	▪ advertisements
▪ musical compositions	▪ maps
▪ choreography	▪ technical drawings
▪ applets	▪ songs
▪ Web pages	▪ images

Figure 6-1 Many different kinds of creative works qualify for copyright protection.

Property Clause of the U.S. Constitution, initially enacted as the Copyright Act of 1790 (Patry, 1994). The Copyright Act of 1976 is the basis of current copyright law (United States Code, 2003). Advancements in technology and the Internet result in the law being revised continually to reflect current needs and issues. Copyright assures that the original creator of the work can do with the work whatever he or she wants. The original creators have the right to authorize someone else to use the work, prohibit others from using their work, or sell their copyright to someone else. This means that they can give up their rights (usually for a negotiated fee) to someone else, who then becomes the copyright owner. This new owner becomes protected by copyright law, as was the original owner.

Copyright law regulates more than just "copying" the work. It also controls translating the material into another language, performing the material (as in a play), copying electronic versions of a work (as in music or movie CD or DVD), and broadcasting it (on radio or TV). In short, copyright covers reproducing a work in any way. Copyright laws protect creators of original works by assuring that they receive their due recognition and economic rewards associated with their creation.

Once an individual or a group creates an original work, this work is considered to be copyrighted simply by its existence. Although copyright is not dependent upon registration, creators of original material can document their ownership by registering a work with the United States Copyright Office. The copyright symbol © is used to identify a copyrighted work. Copyright protection is documented, for a fee, to the originator of the expression for a specified time limit, such as life of the originator plus several years to allow the originator's heirs the benefit of gaining benefit from the copyrighted work (University System of Georgia Board of Regents, n.d. [a]). Documenting a copyright protects the owner of the work by allowing him or her to sue another individual who uses the work without appropriate permission. The exact copyright terms can be complicated and depend on several factors, including when the work was published and created.

When a copyright expires, the work is transferred into the **public domain.** The time after which a copyright expires depends on the type of work, its publication date, and other factors. When the work moves to the public domain, it is no longer protected by copyright and anyone can use it. Information-literate individuals ensure that they do not have to obtain permission to use originally copyrighted materials by checking with the United States Copyright Office to get a specific copyright expiration date for the material in question. And regardless of copyright status, it is courteous and professional to credit the original creator (University System of Georgia Board of Regents, n.d. [b]).

Fair use means that, in some cases, you can copy and distribute copyrighted materials without permission of, or payment to, the copyright holder. In general, fair use allows some limited copyrighted materials for educational, research, and other purposes. Fair-use laws are complicated and not clearly defined. The information-literate individual seeks clarification of the law when he or she is uncertain.

PLAGIARISM

Using someone else's original work without acknowledging the original creator is termed **plagiarism.** The work can be an idea, actual language, or some other original material. Plagiarism is a growing problem in educational and professional settings, and information-literate individuals take care to avoid this unethical and illegal practice.

Examples of plagiarism are

- copying another person's work and submitting it as your own
- presenting work completed by someone else as your own
- taking an idea from someone else and submitting it as your own
- copying text into an original document without indicating the text with quotation marks or correctly acknowledging the original creator of the work

- too closely paraphrasing someone else's work and submitting it as your own
- writing down words spoken by someone else in a face-to-face or telephone discussion and submitting them as your own without acknowledging the original source
- copying diagrams, photographs, images, charts, tables, clip art, and similar items as your own without giving proper credit
- reusing any media that is in electronic form, such as audio files, video files, applets, and software programs, without giving proper credit to the original creator

Regardless of the type of material, if you present the work of others and do not give them proper credit or cite the source of the work properly, it constitutes plagiarism.

You do not have to document anything that is your original creation or idea. Examples of things you do not have to document are

- your own experiences, observations, insights, thoughts, and conclusions
- your own results from personal observation of an experiment or study
- your own artistic or literary creations such as prose, poems, diagrams, artwork, audio recordings, video recordings, and photographs
- facts that are generally accepted as being true
- common knowledge or observations considered to be common sense
- historical events, myths, and legends

To avoid plagiarizing someone else's information, you can follow several strategies, outlined as follows.

- *Quote.* Using another's exact words is acceptable, but you must copy the exact words, use quotation marks around the quoted words, and properly cite the source. Quotation marks should be used whether the copied words are spoken or written. When you are adding your own words to quoted text, you must put your words in brackets to distinguish them from the quoted material. Adding your own words is necessary sometimes to put the quote in context or to fill in missing words so the entire message can be understood more easily.

- *Paraphrase.* Paraphrasing means rephrasing the words of someone else. It is acceptable as long as the meaning is not changed and the originator is credited properly with a citation. The paraphrase must be accurate, and the source properly cited. Paraphrasing involves more than rearranging the order of words or changing minor elements of a passage. Read the original material and without looking at it, rewrite the content using your own words. If you have to intersperse exact phrases from the original, place these words within quotation marks. The paraphrase is followed by a statement giving credit to the original author. An example of a paraphrase is:

  > According to Smith, when children eat too much sugar, they display abnormal behavior for several minutes and then show significant signs of fatigue and irritation.

- *Summarize.* Summarizing requires condensing a significant amount of someone else's work into a shorter statement or paragraph. This is acceptable as long as the meaning is not changed and the originator is given proper credit with a citation. As with paraphrasing, you read the original information and then try to condense the content without looking. If you have used any exact text, place it within quotation marks. Also, place quotation marks around any special words taken from the original text.
- *Take effective notes.* To reduce the likelihood of plagiarism, it is a good idea to take careful notes so you can remember exactly which ideas are yours and which are someone else's ideas. One way to keep track is to develop a note-taking strategy that includes a notation or symbol for your idea (such as *MINE*) and a notation or symbol for the ideas of the author of the work (such as *AU*). Put all direct quotes in quotation marks. When you take notes, designate *AU* next to facts, quotes (with quotation marks), paraphrased sentences, and summaries of the author's work. When you write down your own insights and thoughts, use *MINE* (or whatever designation you choose). And be sure to clearly label the source of the information on each page of your notes.

- *Save your work.* You can take several measures to maintain the security of your own work. To prevent others from plagiarizing your work, keep copies of your draft work in separate files. For example, rather than revising your original file, save the first draft as draft 1, your second draft as draft 2, and so forth. This will be a reminder that you actually did the work yourself. Save copies of your files in separate places, and make at least one hard copy of your work. Do not allow others to access your computer files.

  You can protect your computer and original work by saving documents as protected files that require a password for access. To protect files in Microsoft Word, go to Tools, Protect Document, and make appropriate selections. There is an option to password-protect the document. Of course, you will have to remember the password so you can open your file. This procedure works in most Microsoft Office applications. Other applications have similar features.

HINT: There should be no difference when considering the intellectual property rights for electronic sources and other resources. The same consideration should be given to intellectual property found on the Internet as with any other information source.

CITING INFORMATION SOURCES

As discussed, to avoid plagiarism and infringement on someone else's intellectual property, you will have to properly cite and document the sources of information in your materials. Even if you do not quote or paraphrase the source directly, if the source contributed significantly to your document, you should properly cite it. In addition to giving appropriate credit to the author, proper citation allows the reader or viewer of your material to go to your sources to obtain additional information or verify your facts. It also shows that you actually conducted sound research rather than randomly providing or fabricating information.

There are many acceptable ways to cite information sources in your writing. Methods for writing citations and reference lists are available in guidelines contained in writing **style guides.** Style guides prescribe exact formats for writing, punctuating, referencing sources within text, and citing sources in reference areas and are revised and updated regularly. Many professions, businesses, and academic institutions prefer or require use of one style over another, and some publishers specify the style you are to use. You should become familiar with the style and follow it consistently.

Common style guides and examples of citations according to each are outlined below. Each style guide specifies exactly how various types of citations are to be structured, including punctuation and use of italics, and how the elements are ordered. The style guides give specific styles for the many different types of resource—books, chapters in books, journals, articles in journals, magazines and magazine articles, newspapers and newspaper articles, review articles, online resources, websites, and most other sources of information. Examples of specific styles are as follows.

APA STYLE

The *Publication Manual of the American Psychological Association* (http://www.apastyle.org) is the style prescribed by the American Psychological Association (APA). This style typically is used in the fields of psychology, health, and social sciences:

Publication Manual of the American Psychological Association, 5th ed. (2001). Washington, DC: American Psychological Association.

Correct APA style for citation of a book with one author:

Author, A. B. (year). *Title of book with one author: Subtitle of book.* Location of publisher: Publisher.

Correct APA style for citation of an article of a journal:

Author, A. B. (year). Title of article within the journal. *Title of Journal, Volume number*, page number range.

Correct APA style for citation of a web page:

Author, A. B. (year). *Title of document.* Retrieved Month day, year, from http://web address (Note: No punctuation follows the web address, to ensure accuracy in retrieving)

MLA STYLE

The *MLA Style Manual and Guide to Scholarly Publishing* is the style guide of the Modern Language Association of America (MLA) (http://www.mla.org). This style typically is used in the fields of arts, literature, and humanities:

Gibaldi, J. *MLA Handbook for Writers of Research Papers*. 6th ed. New York: Modern Language Association of America, 2003.

Correct MLA style for citation of a book with one author:

Author, A. B. *Title of book with one author*. Location of publisher: Publisher, year.

Correct MLA style for citation of an article of a journal:

Author, A. B. "Title of article within the journal." *Title of the Journal,* Volume. issue. (year): page number range.

Correct MLA style for citation of a web page:

Author, A. B. "Title: Subtitle of web page." *Title of web page.* Sponsoring/publishing Agency, if available. Additional description information. Date of electronic publication or date of last revision. Day Month Year of access <http://web page address>

CHICAGO STYLE

The Chicago Manual of Style (http://www.press.uchicago.edu) is published by the University of Chicago Press. This style guide has the widest use overall, including the fields of history and other humanities. The official publication is:

The Chicago Manual of Style. 15th ed. 2003. Chicago: University of Chicago Press.

Correct Chicago style for citation of a book with one author:

Author, First Middle. Date. *Title of Book with One Author*: *Subtitle of Book*. Location of publisher: Publisher.

Correct Chicago style for citation of an article of a journal:

Author, First Middle. "Title of Article." *Title of Journal* Volume, no. (year): page number range.

Correct Chicago style for citation of a web page:

Author, First Middle. "Title of web page." Location: sponsor, n.d. (means no date on the web page) http://web address (accessed Month day, year).

Critical Thinking Question

1. What citation style is used or required at your institution? In your profession?

6

HINT: See the respective style manuals for correct citations of other types of information sources.

INFORMATION AND PRIVACY ISSUES

For the general public, **privacy** means keeping private information out of public view or access. For celebrities and otherwise famous (or infamous) people, privacy means keeping their personal lives out of public view. There is enormous controversy over privacy today, especially when national security is involved. Do the privacy rights of individuals supersede the collective rights of the general public to be safe? Or is it the other way around?

Privacy related to information literacy means that individuals using information should maintain the privacy of other individuals' personal information. The HIPAA (Health Insurance Portability and Accountability Act of 1996) protects your medical information in a variety of ways. The actual act and extensive information on its implementation can be found at the Health and Human Services website (http://www.hhs.gov).

The Privacy Act of 1974 also provides many rights to U.S. citizens. For more information, see the U.S. Department of Justice website (http://www.usdoj.gov)

Privacy rights are becoming increasingly important because, in using the Internet, you make a large amount of information available to anyone who wants to access it. In using a computer, you leave behind a large amount of information about yourself. For example, your computer logs your movement through the Internet, storing information in your browser's history. The cached history reveals every web page you visit. You can erase this information to some extent on your own computer, but if you are connected to a server, the record is maintained, typically without user access. In addition, websites collect a large amount of information from you when you access the site. In general, your computer's information and other demographic information are freely available to anyone who chooses to collect it. Information-literate individuals are aware of this reality and take precautions accordingly.

Critical Thinking Questions

1. Why might public access to your personal medical information be a problem? How could someone else use this information against you?
2. Should the personal rights of individuals be sacrificed for the public right to security? Why or why not?
3. How could someone use your personal information (other than medical information) against you?

INFORMATION AND SECURITY ISSUES

In addition to understanding and abiding by the legal and ethical uses of information, information-literate people follow legal and ethical guidelines associated with receiving, viewing, and transmitting information related to security. Information-literate individuals are aware of the following common security issues facing information users.

COMPUTER SECURITY

Because much of what professionals do with information takes place on a computer and the Internet, these systems must be kept as secure as possible. Maintaining security and following security guidelines help to ensure that the information received and sent is free of harmful software and does not infringe upon others' privacy or copyright rights.

Some guidelines for computer security are the following:

- *Maintain current security protection on your computer.* Protecting your computer and the network alike from incoming viruses (e.g., worms, Trojan horses, malware) and other destructive software programs (e.g., spyware) is vital to your privacy and safety and that of others. Security is achieved by installing and continually renewing security software, keeping operating systems updated with the latest security patches, and staying current on the latest security issues related to computers and the Internet. Operating systems and security programs have features that automatically look for updates on a scheduled basis so you are alerted to updates and issues regularly and promptly. In addition, both spyware and virus programs can be set to regularly check your system for problems. Set updates and checks for both spyware and virus programs to run frequently and regularly.

- *Practice safe e-mailing procedures.* E-mail can bring viruses and other destructive software programs to your computer, especially in attached files. Never open an attached file in an e-mail if you are not sure who sent it to you, or if it looks suspicious in any way. Hackers can send destructive programs through other people's e-mail addresses—even people you know. If you are not expecting an e-mail with an attachment from someone you know, confirm that this person indeed sent it to you before you open it.
- *Protect your computer when using wireless technology.* Many laptop users access the Internet via wireless technology. You must secure your system to protect you from hackers who try to access the information on computers or attempt to read Instant Messages or e-mail by tapping into a wireless network. This is especially easy to do in a public-access wireless hotspot, such as in a coffee shop, hotel, or airport. Hackers can access shared files and read anything on a computer. They also can see the information being transmitted over the Internet. For example, if you are using an unsecured wireless access point in a coffee shop to do a banking transaction and a hacker is sitting at the table next to you, you may be giving up your passwords, account numbers, and other confidential information.
- *Practice safe and ethical networking.* Never access an account except the one assigned to you. Also, never access another person's folders or files without his or her permission.
- *Do not use your work's computer resources for personal activities.* This policy often is enforced in businesses and schools. Whatever you do on an organization's computer system can be viewed and retrieved by system administrators, even if you have deleted the material.
- *Never send or make available on a computer obscene, vulgar, rude, derogatory, discriminatory, or slanderous materials.* This practice is potentially illegal and also is highly unethical and unprofessional. Also, you would be wise not to send or distribute unsolicited e-mail, also known as **SPAM,** even if it is cute, humorous, informative, touching, or harmless. SPAM takes up a lot of time and server space and has no place in the work setting.

- *Do not violate copyright laws.* This means that you should not make copyrighted material available for others to see on a network or send copyrighted materials to others without appropriate permissions. The exception is when the use falls within the fair-use guidelines for certain research and educational activities.
- *Do not violate privacy laws.* If you were to access or make available the private information of others, you would be violating privacy laws. This also means that you should never transmit audio or video clips of others or publish an individuals' pictures without their written permission.
- *Use secure passwords.* Passwords help to secure network and computer access, as well as access to individual folders and files. Be smart about your password selection. Passwords should be difficult to guess. For example, a password consisting of your son's name and birthday is probably easily guessed. A password consisting of meaningless random letters and numbers, such as ffg62thk, is a better choice. Although random passwords are more difficult to remember, they are much more secure. Also, select passwords with both numbers and letters to increase the difficulty of guessing. In many systems (though not all), special characters (e.g., $, %, &) can be used to increase the difficulty. Change passwords regularly and at any time you think someone has discovered your password. Never leave your password list on your computer or in an easily located area.
- *Back up your files.* Even the most diligent, safety-conscious computer users are susceptible to a computer crash. Electronic equipment eventually breaks down. To ensure that a computer crash or system virus infection does not become a crisis for you, back up your important computer files in a safe way and store the backup files in a different and safe location. You can back up files using disks and CD ROMs or DVDs; however, these media also are susceptible to damage and may not last as long as you need the files. A tape backup system is inexpensive and a more reliable option. You also can purchase inexpensive Internet storage space from third-party vendors who allow you to upload and store your files on their servers. Be sure to check the credibility of the vender, though.

  Whatever method you use, store your back up files in a location different from that of your computer or network so if some disaster strikes your building, both your computer and your backups will not be there. For extremely important documents, consider making a hard copy of the file and storing it in a safe place.

Be sure to back up your files often as you are working on a document, and save the drafts of your work as separate files. This procedure will protect you in case your file becomes infected with a virus or gets degraded in some way, in addition to documenting that the work is yours if someone steals (plagiarizes) the material.

- *Be aware of Internet scams.* Internet scams consist of any activity in which someone tries to sell you products fraudulently, tries to gain personal information from you, or attempts to get you to invest in some illegal or nonexistent project. Common Internet scams include illegal online auctions, money offers, work-at-home plans, get-rich-quick schemes, travel and vacation offers, and prizes and sweepstakes. Some of these activities are called "phishing" expeditions and have the goal of getting your money, personal information (social security card number or credit card numbers), and other private information. One example is the unsolicited e-mail that makes an offer and requests your credit card number in return.

REFLECTION QUESTIONS

1. How secure is your own computer system and the network you use daily?
2. What specific security steps do you take currently?
3. How could you improve your security?
4. What security steps or policies are taken at your school? (You may have to do some research.) Are these adequate? Do you feel protected?
5. Can you think of any polices you would recommend to your school?

CRITICAL THINKING QUESTION

1. How might a lack of security in regard to those with whom you work impact you personally? List as many ways as you can.

HINT: Go to http://www.ftc.gov/bcp/conline/pubs/online/dotcoms. htm to view the Top Ten List of fraudulent activities. This government website helps to keep the American public informed about fraudulent Internet activities.

COMMUNICATING INFORMATION

Information-literate individuals have the skills to define the problem or formulate the research question effectively, find and access the information using library and Internet resources, evaluate that information in terms of appropriateness and credibility, and organize the information. The final element of computer literacy is the ability to communicate the information legally, ethically, and effectively to a variety of audiences so it is understood and used for some purpose. Keep in mind that you are attempting to achieve a goal by providing information, and your communication strategies will significantly impact how successfully you achieve your goal. In keeping with the information you have read in this text thus far, you are choosing information and the organization strategies that best support your goal. Now you will be selecting your communication methods in the same manner.

In general, effective communication encompasses a multitude of skills sets including

- writing effectively, using various formats and for different purposes
- communicating verbally to individuals and both large and small groups
- using various communication technologies wisely
- presenting information logically and professionally

THE COMMUNICATION PROCESS

To engage in effective communication, several steps in the communication process must take place successfully (see Figure 6-2). These steps apply to communication in general, and are especially important when communicating professional information. In professional communication, additional considerations are appropriate, as outlined.

Step 1: Encode the message. In the first step of the communication process, the sender of the message encodes the message appropriately so the receiver can understand it. When communicating

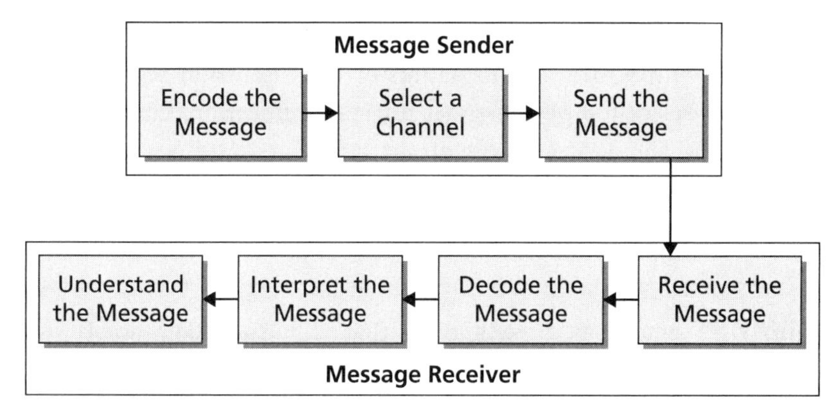

Figure 6-2 There are several components to successful communication involving both the sender and receiver of the message.

professional information, encoding the message effectively is demonstrated by preparing information in a style and at a level that your audience can understand. To do this, the sender must understand the unique characteristics of the receiver (audience) and the purpose of the message.

Step 2: Select a channel. Channels of communication are methods of delivering a message. Channels include written forms such as letters, e-mails, memos, proposals, reports, and online discussions or chat. Verbal channels include face-to-face discussions, small-group presentations, large-group presentations, and telephone discussions. Channels must be selected carefully in light of the audience or receiver of the information, type and sensitivity of the information, and timeframe in which the information must be received and addressed.

For example, to report to a supervisor on sensitive information that impacts another employee or the business operation, a face-to-face discussion with the supervisor or a confidential written report might be the best channel. To provide nonsensitive information that includes charts and graphs and is needed immediately for decision making, an Excel spreadsheet or Word document could be attached to an e-mail. To ensure a written record of all conversation or thoughts in a group discussion, the conversation might be conducted through an e-mail or online discussion thread or blog.

Some individuals are not accustomed to using the computer for communication. If this is the case, an e-mail attachment might not be the best channel. Other people travel extensively, so the cell phone may be the best option for immediate communication, perhaps followed up with written confirmation of the discussion via letter or e-mail. To select the best channel for communication, consider the characteristics and preferences of the audience or receiver, type of information, urgency, need for documentation, and amount and purpose of the information.

HINT: In some cases, more than one channel of communication is prudent. For example, a telephone call can meet immediate, timely needs and a follow-up e-mail will document or back up the initial message delivery.

Step 3: Send the message. For a message to be received as intended, the message must be sent. This sounds simple and obvious, but any sender of a message has to ensure that the message was actually sent. This can be done in several ways or through different channels. For example, most e-mail systems include a feature that provides notification when a message is sent. Or you can confirm that an e-mail was sent by checking the "Sent" box. Important reports that are time-sensitive should be sent via some certifiable delivery service, such as UPS, FedEX, or the U.S. Postal Service. Various processes are available to document and track package delivery. When using verbal channels, the message sender is responsible for actually delivering the message clearly and in an understandable form, free of distractions. (More will be discussed shortly about the various strategies for effective communication.)

Step 4: Receive the message. The sender of the message is responsible for ensuring that the message is received. The receiver must be physically able to hear or read the message in the form in which it was sent, which means that the sender has to select the message channel appropriately. When transmitting professional information, you should consider any adaptation necessary to meet the needs of constituents with disabilities. In most cases, individuals will inform you if they need accommodations of any kind.

Step 5: Decode the message. If the receiver receives the message but cannot decode it, the communication has not been successful. For example, if a message was sent electronically over the Internet in a format that the receiver's computer does not recognize, the receiver will not be able to decode the message. The sender must select the appropriate format—to send the message in a file that is readable by the sender or to provide reader software or a converter (for example, a PowerPoint viewer) with clear instructions on how to download and install the tool. People who communicate via the Internet by either placing information on web pages or e-mailing large files often encounter this difficulty. One solution is to convert files into .pdf files and then provide the link and instructions for how the receiver can view the file by downloading and installing Acrobat Reader. Other issues associated with decoding include language of the message, level of technical jargon and concepts in the message, accessibility by persons with disabilities, and physical appearance of the message.

Step 6: Interpret the message. Once the receiver decodes the message, it must be interpreted accurately. Individuals employ a variety of methods to interpret the meaning of a message. Body language, tone of voice, word selection and sentence structure, and appearance of the message or channel—all impact the interpretation. For example, if a person delivers an important message in a face-to-face discussion or a group presentation and fidgets nervously, refuses to make eye contact, and behaves in an insecure manner, the message might be interpreted as being dishonest. The message receivers, then, may interpret the message to be inaccurate. (More will be discussed about body language and its impact on the message shortly.)

Step 7: Understand the message. Finally, the receiver must understand the message. Again, this is the responsibility of the message sender. The message must be presented clearly in a manner that the receiver can understand. For example, a physician who presents to a patient a highly technical explanation of a disease and its treatment may risk the patient's misunderstanding the information. A teacher who explains information poorly risks being misunderstood by students. A poorly written manual leads to readers' misunderstanding. To ensure that the message is understood fully, the understanding has to be verified in some way.

HINT: As a sender of information, remember that you, not the receiver, have most of the responsibility for successful communication.

step-by-step

Step 1: Encode the message.

Step 2: Select a channel.

Step 3: Send the message.

Step 4: Receive the message.

Step 5: Decode the message.

Step 6: Interpret the message.

Step 7: Understand the message.

- What is the purpose of the communication?
- Who is the audience?
- What are the unique characteristics of the audience?
- What is the environment of the communication?
- What is the urgency of the message?
- What is the best channel for sending the message?
- Has the message really been sent? How do I know?
- Can the receiver receive the message?
- Did the receiver receive the message? How do I know?
- How did the receiver interpret the message?
- Did the receiver fully understand the message? How do I know?

6

CHANNELS OF COMMUNICATION

Each of the numerous channels of communication is appropriate for different types of messages and circumstances of communication. In the workplace, certain channels of communication are used more commonly than others. The channel(s) should be selected based on its ability to facilitate effective communication.

Communicating in Writing

Organization of information in written formats is the topic of chapter 5. Here, examples of common written forms of communication and the situations in which each is best utilized are specified.

- *Memos.* Use a memo in situations when you have to communicate information that informs, supplies facts, asks for information or clarification, confirms, documents, responds, or gives simple directions. Memos are a common form of communication with colleagues within a company or organization. Always complete the To, From, and Date headings at the top of a memo. The "Subject" heading provides the topic of the memo so it can be retrieved efficiently at a later time. Memos are considered more informal than some other formats, so a conversational tone is appropriate. Be direct and concise, and focus on a single topic or subject. Bullets and other visual aids contribute to reader understanding. Memos usually are fairly brief. If additional documents are necessary to clarify the memo, include them as attachments and indicate "attachment" in the heading of the memo.

- *Letters.* Letters are best used for communicating information to those outside of an organization or business. Letters provide permanent documentation of information. They typically are more formal than memos and should be labeled and kept confidential when they include sensitive or private information. Letters can be used to request information in your information search, to document and inform, to reply to requests or questions, and to persuade. Write letters clearly and concisely, always with a positive, professional, and courteous tone. Organize the letter with an opening, a body, and a closing. Always date your letters and sign them manually.

- *Reports, proposals, and papers.* Reports, proposals, and papers are best used for communicating larger amounts of information. Different kinds of documents adhere to specific formats that facilitate achieving the documents' goals. Chapter 5 included a discussion of the organization of common documents in the workplace. In addition to the format, these types of communication channels should be created in a logical, professional, concise, and clear manner to ensure that the reader interprets and understands the information accurately. These documents normally include a variety of visual organizers, such as charts, graphs, timelines, outlines, diagrams, images, and so forth, to support the information.
- *Logs and journals.* Logs and journals can be used to effectively communicate and document information, especially when the research process is ongoing over a period of time. Journals and logs help to document the chronological order of events or observations. Typically, these types of documents are created using an informal tone. When making entries into journals and logs, include the date, time, and circumstance, and be clear and concise. Also, consider using diagrams and other visual elements to organize the information so it can be extracted effectively later if needed to incorporate into a more formal presentation of information.
- *Instructions.* In many instances in the workplace, professionals are required to turn information into logical instructions that others can easily follow. When writing instructions, follow the guidelines below to ensure that the message is clear and understandable.

—Provide a brief introduction telling the reader the purpose or goal of the instructions, who should read the instructions, and in what circumstances the instructions should be used.

—Provide any warnings about safety or security or what *not* to do.

—Start instructions for equipment by giving a clear description (or including a diagram or photograph) of the actual equipment.

—Write the instructions in the proper sequence.

Poor instructions: *First, set the channel. But, before you do, set the time.*

Effective instructions: Set the time. Set the channel.

—Clearly identify the steps in the procedures using numbers or bullets.

Poor instructions: Set the channel, and then the time. Then push the start button.

Effective instructions: Step 1: Set the channel. Step 2: Set the time. Step 3: Push the start button.

—Write in a clear, simple, and concise manner. Omit any unnecessary words or descriptions.

—Write in an active, imperative form (as a command) rather than passive tense.

Poor instructions: First the channel should be set. Then the time should be set.

Effective instructions: Step 1: Set the channel. Step 2: Set the time.

—Test the instructions before giving them to others. Consider having someone else test the instructions as well.

—Give tips for troubleshooting, and identify common mistakes.

—Include diagrams for complicated instructions.

Communicating Visually

Many people are highly visual and learn best when they can see the information. Presenting information visually, then, is a highly effective form of communication for a lot of people. The chapter 5 discussion includes several tips on visually organizing information. Our focus now turns to several methods for communicating visually in the workplace.

- *Poster presentations.* A poster presentation is a static, visual medium used to present information to a large number of people over a period of time. A poster presentation contains the same basic elements as an oral presentation, but the poster itself does the presenting. There should be no need to speak when using a poster, except perhaps to answer any questions from those who view it. A poster presentation is a commonly used format for presenting research information at professional conferences so as many informational presentations as possible can be accommodated. A conference allots a limited number of slots for oral presentations, and rooms often are set up for poster presentations to allow more information to be presented formally.

Most organizations hosting professional conferences and meetings provide specific guidelines for poster presentations in terms of their size, required elements and materials, and so forth. In general, a poster presentation follows the same format as an oral presentation—title, author names and biographical information, abstract, introduction, literature review, methods, results, discussion of results, conclusions, and references. (These elements are discussed in detail in chapter 4.)

- *Drawings and diagrams.* In many cases, information is best presented using a drawing or diagram. Pages of words may be required to convey the same information as a simple diagram or drawing. You do not have to be an artist to produce an effective diagram. Many computer applications enable the creation of excellent diagrams. To develop an effective diagram, consider sketching the information on paper before using a software tool. Clearly label all elements, and include a meaningful title or caption for the drawing. Use color, fills, various sizes of lines and arrows, and automatic shapes commonly found in the software packages.

HINT: To quickly see the various drawing tools available in programs such as Word or PowerPoint, go to the View menu and select Toolbars. Select Customize. Click on the various categories to see the kinds of tools that can be used for different drawing and diagramming purposes. You can drag the specific command icons directly to your toolbar by clicking and dragging the command to your toolbar.

Examples of easy, inexpensive drawing and diagram software:

- Microsoft Word
- Microsoft PowerPoint
- Microsoft Visio
- SmartDraw
- ConceptDraw
- Chartist
- ChartSmith
- Flow

- *Images.* In some cases, the best way to communicate information is through an image. Images can be downloaded, printed, and sent electronically. Information-literate individuals understand the common file formats for communicating information effectively using images.

—*PDF file format*: PDF (Portable Document File) is a portable document format developed by Adobe for viewing files in PDF formats. Adobe provides the Acrobat Reader ("Read Only") without charge. To create or revise PDF documents, however, you must purchase PDF creator software.

Acrobat Reader is ideal for most of your purposes because you can view the image but cannot manipulate it. It is downloadable and viewable by most browsers and other software. Almost any type of file can be converted to PDF format. These files can be of high quality and typically reproduce well.

—*JPEG file format:* The Joint Photographic Exerts Group (JPEG) format is an excellent format for storing and displaying color and grayscale images. JPEG images provide excellent quality while keeping the file size to a minimum. The JPEG file format is good for sending images over the Internet or embedding into other documents.

—*GIF file formats:* The Graphics Interchange Format (GIF) is another format that is commonly used for graphics on the Internet, because you can view this format with most browsers. This format is not the best choice for embedding into business documents, however, as it does not compress well.

Reflection Questions

1. What communication channels do you see yourself using most in your own field of study and future professional position?
2. How would you rate your ability to use these channels professionally and effectively?
3. How can you improve?

—*TIFF file format:* The Tagged Image File Format (TIFF) is versatile. Though the TIFF format requires a specific viewer, most PCs are prepackaged with a basic TIFF viewer. Large TIFF files require broadband Internet connections to be sent effectively over the Internet.

Communicating Verbally

Obviously, people use verbal forms of communication every day, and they are important in the workplace. Most professionals are required to present information verbally in a variety of situations including one-on-one discussions, small-group meetings, large-group presentations, and other settings. Some strategies for fostering successful verbal communication are included here.

In face-to-face situations, people both see and hear you.

- *Face-to-face communication.* In face-to-face situations, people both see and hear you. The impression you make on the recipients of your messages greatly influences the meaning and interpretation of the information. Your impression will depend on your appearance, your behavior, and your use of language. An advantage of face-to-face communication is that you can see the other persons and adapt your message or clarify your meaning easily in response to their nonverbal reactions. Making a positive impression is important, regardless of the purpose of the communication or the information being communicated. Here are some strategies:
  - *Maintain a professional appearance.* Attire should be appropriate to the situation, and you should always maintain good grooming.
  - *Be enthusiastic and attentive.* The demeanor with which you present yourself sets the stage for the message and success of the communication.
  - *Use effective body language.* Body language refers specifically to your nonverbal behaviors, which send powerful messages to others. If your body language disagrees with your words, the receivers are likely to mistrust or misunderstand the information you are conveying. When there is a discrepancy between verbal and nonverbal communication, listeners tend to believe and respond to the nonverbal messages.

    Effective body language includes facing the person you are talking to, making eye contact, using good posture, and maintaining a relaxed state. Avoid body language that suggests you are angry, distracted, uninterested, fearful, lying, or nervous. Be aware that body language can be interpreted differently depending on a person's cultural background. For example, certain hand gestures that are widely accepted in the United States are considered obscene in other cultures. Be aware of different interpretations and be conscious of your nonverbal actions and gestures.
  - *Use excellent listening skills.* When communicating face-to-face, effective listening skills serve several functions. First, attentive listening shows that you are involved in the discussion and are interested as much in what others have to say as in what you are saying. To demonstrate that you are listening, ask questions of

clarification, make eye contact, nod your head in agreement, avoid interrupting, and summarize or paraphrase what is being said by restating the information in your own words.

From a listener standpoint, pay attention to the other person's body language and use the information to your advantage. Be organized in your listening by forming mental images, keeping track of salient points and questions (in writing, if necessary), maintaining an open mind, and asking questions appropriately. Listen to the other person's entire presentation before formulating your own questions so you do not miss significant information. In some cases, this may take practice and discipline, but the impact of effective listening is powerful and contributes to successful face-to-face interactions.

- *Analyze and minimize barriers to communication.* Barriers to communication include language barriers, significant difference in levels of educational or technical expertise, distractions, bias and prejudice, and barriers caused by internal stress, fear, or insecurity. Identify barriers, and do what you can to minimize them. If there is noise or another distraction, move the conversation to a different area or shut a door.

  Language barriers are remedied by translators. For barriers involving differences in education or levels of expertise, you can learn to adjust your words and content appropriately. In situations where you are providing highly technical information to someone who has less training or expertise in the area, avoid using technical jargon, or define and explain technical terms clearly using common terms, analogies, or diagrams as needed. Critically analyze your own biases, prejudices, and assumptions. Being aware of your internal thinking is the first step in eliminating or controlling these hindrances.
- *Avoid assumptions and stereotyping.* We all make assumptions and stereotype people at times. The problem is that not all individuals fit into a group. For example, many people stereotype older individuals as having no interest or skills in high-tech areas when, in reality, many older individuals are highly skilled and knowledgeable in technical areas. Rather than making incorrect assumptions, ask direct questions to establish an accurate picture, and then proceed accordingly. As an example, when you are presenting technical information to a group and

you do not know the level of expertise of the group, simply ask the listeners. They will appreciate your questions and reward you with honest information that will allow you to present the information in a way they can best appreciate and understand.

- *Small-group meetings.* In many workplaces, information is presented in a small-group meeting format. An information-literate individual understands the dynamics of small-group situations and knows how to make informational presentations skillfully. As with face-to-face interactions, understanding the individuals in the group is necessary to communicate effectively with them. What is their level of expertise, and how much do they know about your presentation already? What is their interest in your information? What is their attitude about the information? What is the purpose of the meeting in general? This information should be ascertained prior to the meeting, or at least before beginning your presentation. Also, as with face-to-face interactions, body language, appearance, and demeanor make the first impression, which has a significant impact on the interpretation and understanding of the message.

©2007 JupiterImages Corporation

In many workplace situations, information is presented in small-group meeting formats.

To present information to a small group effectively, consider the timeframe allowed for your presentation. Typically, small-group meetings are brief, and most people cannot or will not sit for a long time without breaks. Make sure that your presentation is well-organized, visual (because many people are highly visual learners), to the point, and clearly presented. Provide a meeting agenda or outline of what you will be saying. Consider providing a brief handout containing bullets or other brief highlights of your information.

When presenting highlights from a lengthy report, distribute copies of that report to all meeting members, with a one-page introduction, summarizing the content, as a cover page. Depending on the topic, consider using PowerPoint or some other visual-presentation software to make your presentations interesting, and present supporting information in the form of charts, graphs, images, and other visual organizers when they will be helpful.

A small-group setting is typically less formal than a large-group presentation, so take advantage of the opportunity to answer questions, listen to different perspectives, and utilize other expertise or experience in the room. Develop a positive rapport with individual group members by acknowledging their strengths and experiences, asking them questions directly, watching and responding to their body language cues, and listening attentively to what they have to say. In advance of your presentation, anticipate their possible questions and be prepared with answers. Either answer the questions as part of your presentation, or bring up your own questions at the end. Listeners will appreciate that you have addressed your information from multiple perspectives and are willing to keep an open mind about the material.

- *Large-group presentations.* Most professionals are required, at one time or another, to make an informational presentation to large groups of people at business gatherings, conferences, professional meetings, and training sessions. Although this type of presentation may be daunting, skill in making large-group presentations is vital to career success. Many of the same rules and guidelines for smaller groups work in presentations to large groups. Make a good first impression. Prepare diligently, including anticipating potential questions and how you will answer them. Know your audience well, and adapt your information to meet their collective needs. Present the information in a highly organized fashion and use visual aids as appropriate to meet the learning style of audience members. Speak clearly, loudly (so the back rows can hear), and maintain eye contact with as many people in the audience as you can. Work to become be relaxed, confident, and enthusiastic.

Most professionals are required to make presentations to large groups of people at some time in their career.

One way to develop rapport with individuals in the audience is to arrive early at the presentation venue and greet as many people as possible as they come into the room. Network with as many individuals as possible to learn their names, why they are there, what they do, and the level of expertise or any special skills or knowledge they might have. Incorporate this information in your presentation if appropriate. Attendees will appreciate being acknowledged, and you will achieve positive rapport with the group. As with small groups, watch body-language cues and adapt accordingly. For example, if people look confused, acknowledge the difficulty of the topic and explain it in a different way.

In very large groups, such as presentations at conferences, visual aids must be carefully planned and executed to be maximally effective. For example, when using a projector for a PowerPoint presentation, the projected image becomes larger and lighter as you move the projector back from the projection surface. Conversely, the image becomes darker and smaller as the projector is moved closer to the projection surface. If you

Reflection Questions

1. Rank your skill level at giving verbal presentations. What are your areas of strength and weakness?
2. What can you do to improve on your weaknesses?
3. When might you be required to make verbal presentations in your job? How important will this be to your career success?
4. In ten years, do you think you will have advanced in your career to a position where you make more presentations? What skills will you need in your field?

Critical Thinking Questions

1. Why do you think so many people are terrified of speaking in public?
2. What can individuals do to get over this fear?
3. What impact do you think a lack of presentation skills might have on a person's career advancement? Why?

are giving a presentation using PowerPoint, the projector must be positioned so the image is both large and dark enough to be easily seen by viewers in the back of the room. This and other considerations are affected by the configuration and size of the room and available equipment. Assessment of the presentation environment and careful adaptations to the environment have a significant impact on how the information is received.

Tips for Making Effective Informational Presentations

- Be well prepared and know your subject well.
- Practice your presentation ahead of time.
- Develop a rapport with as many people as possible as they arrive at the presentation.
- Ensure that you look professional in terms of appearance, cleanliness, fashion, and demeanor.
- Maintain eye contact with as many audience members as possible.
- Smile often, and be enthusiastic and energetic about your topic.
- Speak slowly, clearly, and spontaneously. (Never read your script or notes!)
- Avoid annoying mannerisms, such as clicking a pen, jingling pocket change, twirling your hair, touching your face, unnatural arm movements, etc.
- Avoid hiding behind a podium.
- Avoid talking to a board, slide, or other visual aid and turning back to the audience.
- Introduce yourself and the presentation including why you are qualified to speak about the information.
- Ensure that your presentation is organized in a logical manner.
- Use visual presentations and organizers, but do not read directly from slide presentations.
- Before the presentation, check your visual aids carefully for mistakes.
- Check any equipment you will be using to ensure that it is working properly.
- Become familiar with your presentation room and rearrange if possible and necessary.
- When using electronic files or media, always have a backup file.
- Always have a non-technological back-up plan to technology.
- Vary the nature of your content to engage and interest the audience.

Tips for Effective Presentations

Teaching and Training Situations

At some point in your career, you may be required to use the information you find to teach or train someone. Teaching is a highly specific but useful communication skill that is worth the effort to develop fully. In the workplace, managers, supervisors, mentors, and experienced workers find themselves being asked to train others. Several important strategies for effectively training others are as follows.

©Digital Vision

Many professionals are required to use information to teach or train someone else.

- *Be aware of different learning styles.* The various people with whom you have contact have individual learning styles. Be sure that you can address the visual, auditory, and kinesthetic learner in your training. Most people teach naturally in the style with which they learn best themselves. Make an effort to develop your teaching skills in the other styles so you can meet the needs of all members of your audience effectively.
- *Acknowledge the existing knowledge, skills, and experience of the learners.* All adults come to any training situation with some level of knowledge, skill, and experience. Utilize the previous experience of learners in your training. When trainers do not acknowledge participants' existing knowledge or past experiences, they can hinder the learning experience by appearing condescending.
- *Recognize that adults have to be self-directed.* Though children have to be guided closely in their learning experiences, adults need more control over the learning situation. As a trainer, keep open communication about the goals of the training and include the learners in developing the training plan and activities. The more that adults are invested in the design of their learning, the more they will learn.
- *Realize that adults tend to have more difficulty with memory than younger learners do, especially in new areas.* As we age, our memory tends to diminish. This does not reflect intellect or ability but should be recognized in training situations. To overcome memory obstacles, provide "cheat sheets," checklists, outlines, diagrams, and other visual aids that the learners can take home or to the workplace to remind them of steps, tips, and other significant points.
- *Understand that adults are busy.* Adults go to training events because they have to. They either need new information and skills or they need to document periodic training and professional

development. Recognize this by making excellent use of the training time. Avoid giving "busy work," rambling and getting off-track, and providing unnecessary information. Stick to the main points of the topic. Focus on how to apply information and use it in authentic situations. Reinforce why the information is important, and help learners apply the information to their individual situations.

- *Know that adults tend to be problem-oriented.* Provide hands-on, problem-based activities. Frame the information in a way that helps learners solve problems and find practical ways to apply the information.
- *Recognize that adults are sometimes skeptical of the speaker's credibility.* Members of a training group often internally question the trainer's qualifications for teaching the information. Overcome this by introducing yourself in a way that shows you know your material, have experience or knowledge of the material, and are qualified to conduct the training. Speak with confidence. Avoid mannerisms indicating that you are insecure or nervous. Tell first-hand stories, if possible.
- *Verify that the learner has understood the information.* Throughout the training session and at the end of the session, make sure the training participants understand the information. Watch body language cues. Ask them directly if they understand. Pay close attention to questions that give clues about participants' levels of understanding. If you find that the participants do not understand the information, explain it in a different way—rephrase it, use an analogy, or draw a diagram on the board. Work with participants to pinpoint specifically where they are missing the points.
- *Allow time for people to respond to your questions.* A common mistake by teachers and trainers is to ask a question and then to answer it if no one in the group responds immediately. It takes some time to hear a question, comprehend what is being asked, process the information, formulate a response, then summon the courage to actually respond in a group setting. Allow participants time to do this. Some trainers count to 20 before answering their own question. If you see that no one is going to respond, ask the question in a different way or provide a hint instead of answering it yourself.

6

REFLECTION QUESTIONS

1. In what situations during your career might you be asked to teach or train?
2. How well do you think you will be able to do this?
3. How can you develop these skills or improve the ones you have?

Communicating Electronically

Information can be transmitted effectively in many ways using electronic communication tools. These tools provide the major benefit of transmitting messages immediately over distances. The capacity to attach documents, link to additional information, use multimedia, and include several people in a discussion adds to the functionality of electronic communication tools. Among the electronic communication tools commonly used are e-mail, online chat, and online discussion threads or blogs.

- *E-mail.* E-mail has become an essential communication tool in the workplace. Most professionals have access to e-mail, and many have multiple e-mail accounts. To use e-mail effectively, here are several guidelines:

  Rule #1: Do not use ALL CAPS. This is apt to be interpreted as electronic shouting and is difficult to read. (An occasional word in all capital letters can add emphasis if used sparingly.) Write e-mails in the same way you do other correspondence.

  Rule #2: Check for mistakes. As with any form of communication, the appearance of an e-mail makes an impression that can positively or negatively impact how the message is interpreted. Ensure that your e-mails are professional, free of typographical and grammatical errors, and well-written.

  Rule #3: Complete the subject line accurately. Many people receive numerous e-mails each day and use e-mail correspondence to document conversations, decisions, and information. Title your e-mails appropriately and accurately in the subject line. A meaningful subject line points out the significance of the e-mail message. "No subject" is easily ignored as part of the e-mail filtering process, particularly if the recipient is unfamiliar with the sender.

  Rule #4: Do not send SPAM. SPAM is unsolicited e-mail, and a person probably could spend all day reading, resending, and forwarding the humorous, political, touching, and informative e-mails that arrive at every computer. In the professional world, avoid sending e-mails that are not related specifically to work. Aside from the high risk of offending others, many companies maintain policies against using work e-mails for activities that are not work-related. SPAM also wastes significant workday time.

Rule #5: Do not reply to an e-mail unprofessionally. Do not answer an e-mail when you are angry or frustrated. Do not say things in an e-mail that you would not say in a face-to-face situation. The latter is compounded in that e-mails are permanent records, and often read by people other than the intended receiver. Many companies regularly review the e-mails of their employees. Even though you delete an e-mail, a record of the e-mail remains on your computer or company's server. Use e-mail professionally. In some cases, such as when you have to resolve a conflict or provide feedback, face-to-face communication may be a better choice.

Rule #6: Avoid decorating your e-mails. Most e-mail tools allow you to alter the appearance of the e-mail by adding fancy backgrounds, fonts, color, icons, or other elements that are not straight text. Browsers view different elements in different ways. If a browser displays e-mail embellishments differently than they appeared to you, you may be hindering your message by decorating your e-mails.

Rule #7: Avoid replying to all e-mail receivers unless it is purposeful. Although it sometimes is appropriate to reply to all receivers of an e-mail, do this with purpose and consideration. Reply only to the initial sender, if copies aren't necessary, to avoid filling up e-mail accounts unnecessarily.

Rule #8: Stay secure. Ensure that your e-mails are free of viruses, worms, and other destructive programs that can infect other computers. Use Internet and e-mail security software, and keep the software updated.

Rule #9: Choose your words carefully. As with all forms of written communication, words must be selected to convey the meaning you intend. Be concise. Stick to the point. Be logical in your organization. Explain yourself clearly. If you must send large amounts of information via e-mail, consider attaching a file or using an ftp (File Transfer Protocol) site. An ftp site is a place on a server that can hold electronic files. Files can be efficiently uploaded to, downloaded from, and stored indefinitely on the site.

Rule #10: Avoid using e-mail abbreviations. Unprofessional e-mail senders tend to use trendy e-mail abbreviations (e.g., TTFM = ta ta for now; BCNU = be seeing you; ROTFL = rolling on the floor laughing). These only serve to confuse the receiver and are not professional.

- *Online chat, discussion, and listservs.* Online chat and online discussion forums can be useful ways to communicate information. **Online chat** is synchronous, meaning that those in the chat room must be online and logged into the chat room at the same time. Different Internet Service Providers (ISPs) provide public and private online chat features. Online chat is useful for quick communications with those who are online at the same time.

Online discussion forums are useful ways to communicate information. These methods do not require discussion participants to be online at the same time. A **weblog** or a **blog** is an online discussion forum on a web server. Online discussions and blogs can be public—open to anyone who stumbles onto the discussion—or they can be protected with a login code so only invited members can participate. Online discussion forums are effective in communicating some types of information because you can see exactly what each member of the discussion has said and there is a permanent record of the discussion.

A **listserv** is an online mailing list using e-mail that allows widespread e-mailing of material to members of the listserv. Listservs allow information to be distributed to large groups of people quickly. Many professional organizations use listservs to keep their members updated on issues and other information. There are listservs devoted to almost every topic imaginable.

The same etiquette should be used for online chat, discussion, and listservs: Be professional, clear, and courteous. Remember that anything you say is public and permanent.

HINT: Do not say anything online that you would not want everyone you know (or will know in the future) to read.

In the scenario presented at the beginning of this chapter, Ian Smith was asked to conduct research that would provide credible and verifiable information for his business's management team. He was

REFLECTION QUESTION

1. In what ways do you envision that electronic communication will be useful in your career or workplace?

CRITICAL THINKING QUESTIONS

1. How can you see an improperly sent e-mail hurting your career or position in the company? List as many different situations as you can.
2. What are the dangers of using e-mail in the workplace, even if it is used professionally?

asked to present the information to a small group of managers and then again to a larger audience at a business conference. Because Ian knew how to document his research properly during the note-taking and writing process, he was successful at showing his superiors that he used credible information. Anyone on his management team could easily return to the original source of information and verify the facts using the citations that Ian provided in his report. Ian also had developed skills in presenting information to a small group, as well as to a larger audience in a more formal presentation venue. These skills allowed him to come across as relaxed, confident, and highly professional. His success impacted his career advancement positively.

learning activities

Activity #1: Personal Note-taking Procedure

Goal: To develop a personal note-taking procedure that avoids plagiarism when conducting research.

STEP 1: Think carefully about how you can take notes during the research process. Develop a plan of action for your note-taking procedure to help you formalize how you take notes.

STEP 2: Write down this plan in a step-by-step procedure format and place your plan in your portfolio. If you find it useful, create a checklist that will help you follow the plan during any research activity.

Activity #2: Computer Security Evaluation

Goal: To emphasize the importance of computer security and to evaluate the current level of your computer's security.

STEP 1: Develop a checklist for your computer security. Include all relevant steps, programs, and procedures to ensure safe computing, in your personal home office and workspace, as well as in your workplace.

STEP 2: Use your checklist to evaluate the security level of your current situation.

STEP 3: Develop a plan to optimize your security situation in any place you use your computer.

Activity #3: Citation Exploration

Goal: To demonstrate an understanding of how to cite information sources properly.

STEP 1: Determine the acceptable style used by your institution or workplace for citing information sources.

STEP 2: Search the Internet for information on using this style.

STEP 3: Acquire the official style guide and implement use of this style in each assignment, research task, and other written document.

Activity #4: Presentation Checklist

Goal: To acknowledge the importance of presentation skills in a variety of situations and to develop a tool that can be used to develop presentation skills.

STEP 1: Develop a detailed checklist that can be used to evaluate your skills in presenting information. Categorize the checklist by face-to-face interactions, small-group interactions, and large-group presentations. Be as detailed as possible, and include all aspects of the presentation. Conduct additional research as necessary to get additional ideas to include in your checklist.

STEP 2: Organize a group of classmates or colleagues and ask them to review your checklist (or review each the checklists of each member of the group.)

STEP 3: When you are asked to make various presentations, ask a classmate to use the checklist to give you a constructive critique of your presentation. Alternatively or in addition, videotape your presentation and use the checklist to critique yourself.

STEP 4: Based on the feedback, develop a personal plan for improvement. Consider selecting one area at a time. Practice makes for excellent presentation skills. Without feedback, improvement is difficult. As difficult as it may be to receive constructive criticism, developing these important professional skills is essential.

LEARNING OBJECTIVES REVISITED

Review the learning objectives for this chapter and rate your level of achievement for each objective using the rating scale provided. For each objective on which you do not rate yourself as a 3, outline a plan of action that you will take to fully achieve the objective. Include a timeframe for this plan.

1 = did not successfully achieve objective

2 = understand what is needed, but need more study or practice

3 = achieved learning objective thoroughly

	1	2	3
Explain how privacy and security can be breached and protected in both print and electronic environments.	☐	☐	☐
Explain intellectual property, copyright, and fair use of copyrighted material and how they relate to using information legally and ethically.	☐	☐	☐
Explain appropriate ways to participate in electronic discussions.	☐	☐	☐

Steps to Achieve Unmet Objectives

Steps	Due Date
1. ____________________	__________
2. ____________________	__________
3. ____________________	__________
4. ____________________	__________

POTENTIAL ITEMS FOR LEARNING PORTFOLIO

Refer to the "Developing Portfolios" section at the front of this textbook for more information on learning portfolios. Consider adding the following results from this chapter's learning activities or even ideas of your own to your learning portfolio.

- Personal Note-taking Plan
- Computer Security Evaluation Checklist
- Presentation Checklist
- Personal Plan for Improvement of Presentation Skills

REFERENCES

Patry, W.F. (1994). *Copyright law and practice.* Retrieved January 22, 2007 from http://digital-law-online.info/patry/patry5.html

United States Code (2003). *Copyright law of the United States of America and related laws contained in Title 17 of the United States Code.* Retrieved January 22, 2007 from http://www.copyright.gov/title17/

United States Copyright Office. (2005). U.S. Copyright Office: A brief introduction and history. Retrieved September 5, 2006 from http://www.copyright.gov/circs/circ1a.html

University System of Georgia Board of Regents (n.d. [a]). *Giving credit where credit is due.* Retrieved August 31, 2006 from http://www.usg.edu/galileo/skills/unit08/credit08_09.phtml

University System of Georgia Board of Regents (n.d. [b]) *Public Domain.* Retrieved August 31, 2006 from http://www.usg.edu/galileo/skills/unit08/credit08_10.phtml

Conclusion

MOVING ON FROM HERE

You now are familiar with the many elements contributing to your success as an information-literate student and workplace professional. You should come away from the *100% Information Literacy* experience with ideas and strategies for defining the information you need, finding the information by using various library and online resources, evaluating that information critically, organizing the information in a logical manner, and communicating the information effectively in a variety of situations.

For now, practice what you have learned. Remember to keep these concepts and ideas in the forefront of your mind so you can apply them readily to your classroom activities. These strategies are not necessarily easy, so practice is important. With practice, the techniques and methods will become second nature to you. When you enter the workplace, be sure to incorporate these strategies in your daily tasks. You may find that you are the most information-literate individuals in your workplace—which will make you a top asset to your employer.

Again—congratulations on your successes to date and all the best to you as you pursue your goals!

Glossary

A

Abstract: A brief synopsis of the article

Accessibility: How well features are incorporated in a multimedia object, making the site easy to use for those with various disabilities

Aggregators: Vendors of a database

Almanac: A publication that provides statistics, lists, figures, tables, and specific facts in a variety of areas

Alphabetical organization: Organization of information by the alphabet in order from A to Z.

Analyze: To break down complex concepts into parts and then study how the parts are related to each other in making up the whole

Area chart: A visual representation of data displaying trends and their magnitude over time

Atlas: A collection of geographical and historical information

Author search: Locating a library source by a specific author

B

Bar chart (also called **column chart** or **histogram**): A visual representation of data used to compare data by varying the length of the columns or bars

Bias: A viewpoint in which facts are presented with prejudice

Bibliographic items: Pieces of information in a library

Blog: An online discussion forum on a web server

Bloom's taxonomy: A conceptualization of six progressively more complex ways of thinking: knowledge, comprehension, application, analysis, synthesis, and evaluation

Boolean operators: The words "and," "or," and "not" used in combination with keywords to broaden or narrow computer search results by specifying exactly how the search is to be conducted

C

Call number: A label or address assigned to each library item, presenting information to logically organize the item and then physically locate the item in the library stacks

Card catalog: A set of physical file cabinets containing a catalog record with each library item's relevant information, used to physically documented the holdings in a library

Catalog record: A small index card containing each library item's relevant information in a card catalog

Chronological organization: Organization according to time

Citation: (a) An index entry; (b) The source of a fact indicated in the text of an article

Computer literacy: A basic understanding of how a computer works and how it can be used to complete tasks

Concordance: An alphabetical list of the most pertinent words in a given text and a notation of where they might be found within that text

Copyright: Protection of intellectual property such as literary works, artwork, music, audio and video productions, photographs, and newspaper articles

Creative thinking: The process of actively exploring possibilities, generating alternatives, keeping an open mind toward change, and combining ideas to create something new or to view old concepts in new ways

Critical thinking: The mental processes of conceptualizing, applying, analyzing, synthesizing, and evaluating information

D

Database: A collection of digitized information organized for simplified, fast searching and retrieval of information

Dewey Decimal System (DDS): A library classification system designed by Melville Dewey in 1876 to create a uniform and efficient way of organizing information that the public could easily use

Dictionary: An alphabetical listing of words and is used for a quick search of a word or topic to find word meaning, spelling, and pronunciation

Directory: A collection of data organized in a way that allows a user to access the information easily

E

Encyclopedia: A collection of detailed articles on a wide range of subjects

Executive summary: An abstract or brief synopsis commonly found in business proposals and other documents

Exhibit: A supporting document placed at the end of an article

Explain: To make the thought process, facts, or concepts clear

Evaluate: To examine critically, given a specific set of criteria

F

Facts: Things that can be proven to have happened or to exist

Fair use: Specific situations in which a copyrighted work can be legally copied and distributed without permission of or payment to the copyright holder

Fiction: Content based on imagination and not necessarily on fact

Focused research questions: Research questions designed to break down the main questions into more detailed questions directed to the specifics of the topic and purpose of the question

Functionality: The way in which a multimedia element works or functions within the environment in which it is being viewed

G

Gateway: Same as a Web portal

General index: An index that covers a broad range of topics in scholarly journals, popular magazines, and newspapers

GIF File Formats: The Graphics Interchange Format (GIF) format commonly used for graphics on the Internet since the images can be viewed with most browsers

Grant: A workplace document written to obtain funding for research or project

H

Handbooks: Resources that provide concise data, usually in table or chart form on a specialized subject area, commonly used for finding current statistics, procedures, instructions, or specific information on a topic

Hierarchical organization: Organization of information in a specific order, such as from most to least important or least complex to most complex

Higher-order thinking: Levels of progressively more complex thinking from low levels of thinking such as knowing or identifying facts to higher levels of thinking such as analyzing, synthesizing, and evaluating complex information sets

Highlighting: A technique that researchers use to mark important words, phrases, or passages of text for future use

Historical fiction: Information based on an event or sequence of events in history that actually occurred, with people who actually lived or were created within an author's imagination

Home page: The main or first screen of a website with links to other pages on the site

Hypothesis: A statement that a researcher will attempt to support with the results of a specifically designed study

I

Index: An alphabetical list that can be used to find information within a source

Industrial design rights: Protection for the aesthetics or appearance, design, or style of the originator

Industrial property: Intellectual property created in the line of conducting business or for business purposes such as inventions, trademarks, and industrial or business designs

Infer: To draw conclusions from evidence or facts

Information literacy: The skills required to find, access, retrieve, evaluate, use, and communicate information

Information retrieval system: An electronic system that allows access to electronic resources and information

Intellectual property: Anything created by the mind, such as literary works (books, poems, essays), artwork (drawings, paintings), inventions, ideas, logos or symbols, names, designs, and images or photographs

Internet: An electronic network that connects personal computers and organizational computer facilities around the world

Interpret: To comprehend the meaning or significance of something

Invention: Any idea or concept that is new, useful, and not obvious

J

JPEG File Format: The Joint Photographic Exerts Group format used for storing and displaying color and grayscale images

Joint venture publishers: A type of publisher that often charges authors a fee to publish their work and typically limits its role in publication to the actual production of a book rather than copyediting and marketing

K

Key words: A list of terms that help to identify main concepts of an article in a scholarly journal

Keyword search: Computer searching for a library resource using a word related to the topic of the content

L

Library catalog: A log or register of all the items in the library

Library literacy: An understanding of the different kinds of information resources housed in a library, how to access these resources, and how to access the information within these resources

Library of Congress Classification System: A method of organization developed in the early 1900s by the Library of Congress to organize the vast amounts of materials in our nation's library into 21 broad categories and numerous subcategories

Line chart: A visual representation of data displaying a trend over time

Listserv: An online mailing list using e-mail that allows widespread e-mailing of material to members of the listserv

Literature review: The section of a scholarly journal that comes after the introduction section and provides a brief overview of the relevant studies or articles that support or provide background information on the current study

M

Main research question: A research question that is not too broad or narrow, used to focus research appropriately for a topic and audience

Manual: A resource that provides detailed and sometimes "how to" information on highly specific topics

Media literacy: The ability to understand, analyze, evaluate, and produce information in a variety of media-based formats

Metasearch engine: A search engine that searches multiple individual search engines simultaneously

Multimedia: Information in a form other than print

N

Navigation bar: An area of a website that contains links to other pages on the site, or sometimes to entirely different websites

Neutral point of view: A viewpoint in which only the facts are presented without bias

Newspapers: Periodicals that include factual and editorial information on local, regional, national, or international fronts and might be general or topic-specific

Nonfiction: Information presented as fact

Note-taking: A technique that researchers use to organize and abbreviate highlighted or other collected information

O

Online chat: Synchronous communication in which chatters must be online and logged into the chat room at the same time

Online public access catalog (OPAC): A computerized online catalog of all the materials held in a library that can be searched quickly and efficiently using a computer

Opinions: Statements or judgments or beliefs, which may or may not be true

P

Patent: Legal protection of an invention giving the inventor exclusive rights to develop and sell the invention commercially to make a profit for a certain period of time

PDF File Format: A portable document format originally developed by Adobe for viewing files

Peer-reviewed (refereed): Describes scholarly journals that incorporate articles that have been looked at and accepted by experts who are knowledgeable in the topic area

Periodical: A resource published on a regular or recurring basis—daily, weekly, monthly, bimonthly, quarterly, or annually

Periodical index: A cumulative list of articles from periodicals

Pie chart: A visual representation of data showing the contribution of each value to a total (in the shape of a pie)

Plagiarism: The unauthorized use of the words and thoughts of another person, representing them as one's own original work

Plugin: An additional software module that must be installed on a computer to run interactive elements and applets or to display specialized types of data

Popular magazines: Periodicals that provide information on topics of interest to the general public, such as news, entertainment, lifestyles, popular culture, leisure reading, parenting, home, science and nature, self-improvement, and do-it-yourself projects

Poster presentation: A static, visual medium used to present information to a large number of people over a longer period of time than a verbal presentation

Primary information sources: The information sources closest to the actual event, time period, or individual in question

Privacy: Keeping private information out of public view or access

Problem solving: Using a systematic process to find a solution to a question or issue

Proposal: A workplace document typically written to suggest a program or action

Public domain: refers to a published work that no longer is protected by copyright

Publisher: An entity responsible for the actual publication or website in which the information is located

Purpose statement or **Thesis statement:** A sentence toward the beginning of an article that explicitly states the intent of the study or article

Q

Qualitative data: Data that describe the characteristics or observations of something

Quantitative data: Data that measure something

R

Ready reference sources: Materials that usually are kept handy at or near the reference desk in a library because of their frequent use

Refereed: Same as peer-reviewed

Reference desk / Reference Section: An information desk in a library

Reference librarian: The librarian who is specifically responsible for managing information fin the reference area of the library

Reference list: A complete listing of each citation in an article

Reference source: Material from which information can be drawn

Review article: An article written for the sole purpose of discussing the previous literature

S

Scanning: Moving quickly through material to see if it is what is needed

SCANS Report: A document created by the Secretary's Commission on Achieving Necessary Skills, suggesting workplace skills necessary for success in the workplace

Scatter chart (sometimes called a **scatter plot**)**:** A visual representation of data comparing pairs of values under the same situations

Scholarly journal: A periodical that often is published by an educational institution or a professional association and includes articles and reports on original investigations, reviews of literature, and evaluations of industry products

Scope: The broadness or narrowness of a topic

Search engines: Computer software that makes the World Wide Web searchable using keywords or phrases

Secondary information sources: Sources of information that are removed from the primary source

Skimming: Reading in a superficial or cursory manner to quickly determine the main idea in text by reading subheadings and the first sentences of sections and paragraphs

SPAM: Unsolicited e-mail

Style manual / Style guide: An instructional publication that provides guidelines for writing mechanics and documentation format for research papers and theses

Subheadings: Further divisions of subject headings

Subject directory: A collection of links to a large number of Internet resources, typically organized by topic area

Subject headings: Specifically designated terms and phrases designed to organize library materials consistently

Subject search: Locating a library resource using the Library of Congress subject heading

Subject-specific periodical indexes: Indexes that cover articles in selected scholarly journals related to a broad topic or subject area

Subsidy publisher: Same as joint venture publisher

Superintendent of Documents Classification System (SuDoc): A library classification system used by the U.S. Government Printing Office to classify publications

Synthesize: To combine separate thoughts to form a concept

T

Technical report: A workplace document commonly used to communicate results of a project or research

Technology literacy: The ability to use a variety of technologies to find, access, effectively organize, use, and communicate information

Thesaurus: A collection of synonyms, near-synonyms, antonyms (opposite words), phrases, and slang terms for words

Thesis statement. Same as Purpose statement

TIFF File Format: The Tagged Image File Format (TIFF) format used to view image files

Title search: Looking for a library resource by its name

Trademark: A legal protection that helps businesses distinguish their products and services from one another

Trade publication: A periodical published for a specific industry or business, usually published by an association tied to the trade

U

Universal resource locator (URL): An Internet address

Usability: How easy or difficult a multimedia element is used by the intended audience

V

Vanity press: Same as a joint venture publisher

Venn diagram: An illustration using circles that stand alone or overlap to show logical relationships between concepts or ideas

Verifiable: Describes information that is based on facts that can be shown to be true or documented by another or several credible source or sources

W

Web browser: Specific software that allows viewing of a Web page as it is intended to be viewed and allows access to the page's functionality

Weblog: An online discussion forum on a web server

Web page: An electronic resource on the World Wide Web assigned a unique Internet address

Web portal: A site on the Internet that provides links to many different kinds of information

Website: A collection of Web pages stored in a single folder or within related subfolders of a web server

World Wide Web: An international network of Internet servers that allows access to documents written in HTML (hypertext markup language) and provides links to other documents, graphic files, audio files, video files, and many other forms of information

Index

Page numbers followed by a *t* or *f* indicate that the entry is included in a table or figure.

U

V

W